Praise for the 20-30 Something Garden Guide

"Think of Dee Nash as your favorite horticultural big sister. Pretty soon, your thumb will be green and your salad bowl will be filled with tasty greens you've grown yourself."

– Debra Prinzing, author of *Slow Flowers* and *The 50-Mile Bouquet*

"You can't do better than Dee Nash for your personal gardening coach; she's learned from the ground up and knows how to make it fun and rewarding, whether you want to start small or jump right into growing a bountiful harvest of food and flowers."

– Nancy Ondra, author of *Grasses* and *The Perennial Care Manual*

"If you know someone planting their first garden, buy them a copy of this book. It matters not if they have a balcony or a larger backyard growing space, it's all here: the how-tos, the whys, and the whens. Dee lays it out in an easy going style. Along with the book, wrap up a pair of your favorite garden gloves and a pack of lettuce seeds, and you will have launched someone on a lifetime of gardening."

– Mary Ann Newcomer, the Dirt Diva and author of
The Timber Press Guide to Vegetable Gardening in the Mountain States

"An aha! moment on every page. With encouragement, inspiration and practical advice – and three distinct garden plans for gardens of every size – Dee's step-by-step instructions provide a long-term road map for success."

– Rebecca Sweet, author of *Garden Up!* and
Refresh Your Garden Design with Color, Texture and Form

"If you're looking for a book that combines practical food growing experience with innovation, humor and country sense, look no further. Dee Nash is an enthusiastic garden coach who provides the basic know-how and the encouragement for young (and not-so-young) wannabe gardeners to start growing their own food."

– Niki Jabbour, author of *The Year Round Vegetable Gardener*
and *Groundbreaking Food Gardens*

"Where was this book when I was a struggling young gardener? Dee Nash writes with an ease, depth of knowledge and familiarity as only a true, hands-in-the-soil gardener can. I am grateful that Dee is sharing her passion with new generations of gardeners. Carpe terra!"

– Sharon Lovejoy, author of *Trowel & Error*

THE
20-30 something
GARDEN GUIDE

A no-fuss, down and dirty Gardening 101 for anyone who wants to grow stuff

THE

GARDEN GUIDE

A no-fuss, down and dirty Gardening 101 for anyone who wants to grow stuff

DEE NASH

st. lynn's
press

PITTSBURGH

The 20-30 Something Garden Guide
A no-fuss, down and dirty, Gardening 101 for anyone who wants to grow stuff

ISBN-13: 978-0-9855622-7-4

Library of Congress Control Number: 2013941487
CIP information available upon request

First Edition, 2014

St. Lynn's Press . POB 18680 . Pittsburgh, PA 15236
412.466.0790 . www.stlynnspress.com

Book design – Holly Rosborough
Editor – Catherine Dees
Editorial interns – Allison Keene, Claire Stetzer

Photo credits:
Dee Nash – pages xiii, xvii, xviii, xx, 1, 5, 8, 9, 10, 13, 15, 16, 17, 18, 19, 21, 23, 27, 28, 31, 32, 33, 34, 35, 36, 37, 38, 39, 40, 41, 42, 44, 45, 46, 47, 48, 50, 51, 52, 53, 56, 57, 58, 63, 64, 66, 67, 70, 73, 75, 76, 77, 79, 81, 83, 86, 90, 91, 93, 94, 98 (top), 102, 105, 107, 108, 109, 110, 111, 112, 113, 114, 116, 117 (bottom), 119, 120, 122, 123, 124, 131, 132
Claire Nash – pages xiv, 21, 60, 61, 140
Colleen Dieter – pages 6, 97, 99, 125, 126
Kerry Michaels – pages 20, 25
Shawna Coronado – page 54
David Fenton – page 65
Layanee DeMerchant – page 69
Leslie Kuss – pages 74, 121
Helen Johnstone – page 115, 117 (top), 118
Holly Rosborough – pages viii, 22, 62, 65, 68, 82, 84, 96, 104, 127
Paul Kelly – pages 43, 92, 98, 103

Printed in Canada
On certified FSC recycled paper using soy-based inks

This title and all of St. Lynn's Press books may be purchased for educational, business or sales promotional use. For information please write:
Special Markets Department . St. Lynn's Press . POB 18680 . Pittsburgh, PA 15236

10 9 8 7 6 5 4 3 2 1

To Bill, who made all my garden dreams come true.

TABLE OF CONTENTS

TABLE OF CONTENTS

GARDEN 3
A Garden to Delight the Senses

INTRODUCTION

ANYONE CAN BE A GARDENER. You don't need a lot of space to get great results, and you certainly don't have to be an expert. You just have to know a few key things to do and some things not to do. All you need is a step-by-step guide and, ideally, a knowledgeable friend to help you along the way. Have you ever wished someone would just show you how to get started and stand by you?

No one is born with a brown thumb

People often come up to me after talks and at the garden center and say they would love to garden but can't because they have a brown thumb. My reply is that no one is born with a brown thumb, or a green one for that matter. Gardening is a skill learned by trial and error. It could also be compared to a sport like cycling, baseball or running. You need a coach to help you get started and then lead you through the joys and pitfalls everyone experiences. So, abandon the old myth that you are naturally a good or bad gardener. If you want to learn to garden, grab a coach and go for it!

Gardening is one part artistic endeavor and one part craft

I can teach you the craft of gardening. I'm a third generation Oklahoman. In my wild and woolly state, I know something about weather extremes and other difficulties that can plague a garden. As part of the Great American Prairie, Oklahoma's weather is very unpredictable. Those spring storms really do come sweeping down the plains with rain, hail and even tornadoes. While other states enjoy the good old summertime, we face oppressive heat, and in the winter, bouts of extreme cold. Oklahoma gardeners suffer drought just like Texas and Arizona gardeners, and when rainfall does come, it falls in torrents. Perhaps you read about the Dust Bowl in school, or watched Ken Burns' special on PBS, but my grandparents lived it. They grew gardens despite desperate circumstances, and they came through the Great Depression largely due to the produce they grew and the chickens they raised.

Needless to say, I come from hardy stock

I've grown food for as long as I can remember. My earliest memories are of my grandmother's garden, a highly productive vegetable plot with fruit trees and climbing roses in her small, urban backyard. I distinctly remember my white baby shoes contrasted against dark earth as I toddled behind her. I also see my grandfather standing beneath an apple tree, its limbs hanging low with rich, red fruit. Their apple trees grew in a portion of the chicken yard where they raised Rhode Island Red hens. Raising chickens was not a fad. Those chickens ate bugs, like the codling moths that plague apple trees. Each day, they also provided eggs for my grandparents' table.

Although I didn't begin gardening until I started with indoor plants in my teens, my grandparents shared their experience with me. Later, when I moved to my first home, the first thing I planted was a rose. I called my grandmother right after I dug the hole. She was overjoyed because I was carrying on her gardening traditions. Now, I want to pass this knowledge on to you. The artistic side of the gardening experience is something you'll be discovering for yourself.

Food, foliage, flowers…and the artist in you

Gardening takes effort, but in growing your own vegetables, fruit and flowers, you gain far more than the time you put into it. You get outdoor exercise and you learn more about your home, the Earth. You get time away from the computer screen, too. You will also enrich your life in ways you never expected. Nothing beats birdsong in the morning while you water or weed. Nothing.

Why garden?

1. **MONEY.** A packet of seeds will yield a tremendous amount of food or flowers. Any plant you place in the garden produces more fruit than you can imagine. Compare the price of a seed packet with a few bags of produce from the local farmers' market and you'll never completely rely on stores again.

2. **FOOD.** Vegetables and fruits you pick straight from the vine taste better. Because you have control of their growing environment, you know they aren't genetically modified or covered in chemicals. Take care of your garden, and it will, in turn, provide you and your family with fresh produce, much of which can't be bought in stores, especially at the peak of freshness. Grow unique things like goji berries or blueberries. You can in your garden, and they aren't costly like store-bought.

3. **FLOWERS.** Fresh flowers are food for the soul and shouldn't be left out of any garden. Most store-bought flowers have been shipped from far-away countries, where they are laced with chemicals and fumigants, and the companies growing them employ workers who don't earn a living wage. The scent is bred out of many commercial flowers in order to achieve those "perfect," long-lasting blooms. But you can grow natural flowers, scented and beautiful.

4. **BEAUTY.** Intangible benefits are just as important as the more practical ones. A garden – even if it's a deck or patio – is a place to bring forth the artist in you, and to feed your senses. When you consider the almost infinite shapes, textures and colors of plants and containers, and all the ways they can be arranged, your garden space is a canvas just waiting for you.

Tried and true

Maybe you've honestly tried your hand at growing things before, and your garden didn't live up to your expectations. Did squash bugs eat your squash? Did your zinnias develop mildew? Join the club. All gardeners have setbacks. Good gardeners kill plants. Don't be discouraged. Failure means we are stretching our gardening muscles and the limits of our climate. The environment may work against us at times, but that's why we have compost heaps. We turn the remains of our successes, along with our failures, into black gold. Rejoice! It's the circle of life, baby!

With this book, you can create an inviting oasis wherever you live. I know, because I've lived and gardened in all circumstances, from a city apartment with only a south-facing balcony to my present home in the country on 7.5 acres.

Inside, you'll find three, distinct, garden development plans for all sizes of available space – balcony, patio or small yard– along with easy, illustrated steps to take you through three years of building upon success and lessons learned. But no pressure...you can work at your own pace. Work ahead if you like, or take two years (even three!) at a particular stage. It's your garden and your choice. You can also start with the first garden plan, which is all about containers, and then move on to the second garden plan or the third. It's independent study, but with a friend. I'm standing right beside you, celebrating what works and helping with what doesn't.

I should also mention that I've loaded up these pages with how-to's, easy-to-achieve DIY projects, charts, sketches – and lots of tips and other gardening road signs. And we'll kick-start your learning curve with a brief glossary of common garden terms, right up front. Oh, and a gardener's basic tool kit, too. You didn't think I was going to throw you into the deep end without your water wings, did you?

About time

Caring for the garden can be worked around tight schedules, including the 40-plus-hour workweek and the topsy-turvy lifestyle of a new parent – both of which provide little time for the great outdoors. I understand the constraints of a busy schedule. I had three of our four children in six years and also worked full time in an office building. As a result of my own hectic life, I had to learn to work in 30-minute increments. Was it worth it? Absolutely. There was nothing like pulling into my driveway at the end of the day and seeing containers full of flowers by the front door, welcoming me home.

Why am I writing a garden book for 20-30 Somethings? Because those were some of the busiest years in my own life, and because two of my children, Ashley and Megan, are 20-30 Somethings themselves. I understand only too well the challenges of trying to "do it all" and still keep some balance, beauty and connection in our days.

Reality check

Have you been watching (and drooling over) some of those amazing garden shows on TV? Fun as they are, they can leave the impression that gardening is all about DIY projects and instant gratification. You have a garden crew or television crew come in, and in a few hours – voila! The yard is finished. Who wouldn't want that? But what doesn't come across is the reality that gardening is more about the process than the results. Even projects completed by experts must be maintained. Those crews leave and you are alone with their creation.

Clockwise from top:
Bill, Dee, Claire, Ashley, Megan and Brennan

I want a richer experience for you. I want these garden projects to be yours, and to have your ideas inhabit them once the soil and plants are installed. I also want you to try to slow down and consider gardening as the process that it is. Just like yoga, it will give you great results, but it's the ongoing process of inhabiting the postures and learning to breathe that gets you there. And just like yoga, gardening can take you away from the computer or your day job and help you to relax – even if it's just minutes a day.

These are all good reasons to garden, so let's plunge our hands into the soil and get dirty. The garden is our playground. Let's play!

Dee

A GARDENER'S GLOSSARY

Although no garden glossary is complete, below are a few vegetable-growing terms you'll find helpful.

* * *

Aeration – The loosening of soil or other matter by various means, allowing air to pass freely through it.

Acidic Soil – Soil with a pH reading below 7.0; soil measuring above 7.0 pH is called alkaline. Drier soils tend to be more alkaline. Use a soil test to determine pH along with other factors.

Amendment – Organic material added to soil to improve it.

Annual – A plant that completes its entire growth cycle from seed to bloom and again to seed in one year's time.

Beneficial Insects – Insects that improve the soil (e.g., earthworms), pollinate plants, or control harmful insects and other garden pests.

Biennial – A plant that takes two seasons to complete its life cycle, flowering and producing seed in the second year.

Blossom End Rot – A disorder of tomatoes, peppers and eggplant caused by a lack of calcium. Uneven watering and drought are also factors.

Bolting – When a cold-weather plant, like spinach or kale, is stressed by heat, causing it to flower and set seed if left in place. All is not lost: you can eat these flowers, too.

Cloche – A glass or plastic cover meant to protect plants from cold temperatures or animals.

Companion Planting – Growing one or more plants together because they perform well in the same space and benefit each other.

Compost – Organic humus created by layering green and brown matter and allowing them to decompose. Great for the garden, it helps maintain soil moisture and temperature while also balancing soil organisms to prevent disease and improve fertility.

Cultivar – A plant variety or strain produced in cultivation through breeding or selection.

Cutworm – Worm-like larvae of any variety of moth that curls up into a C-shape and cuts plants off at soil level. Often green, brown or yellow with stripes. Various methods are used to foil these creatures when new plants are set out into the garden.

Dormancy – The act of a plant not producing growth and being in a state of stasis. Dormant oils are a natural pest control, sprayed when fruit trees and other perennials are dormant.

GMO – Genetically modified organism, meaning its genetic material is modified using genetic engineering. GMO foods are often a result of gene splicing from two different species.

Heirloom Plants – Time-tested, open-pollinated plants passed down from more than one generation of gardeners often in a particular region – often having more vigor and disease resistance for that region.

Hybrid – Controlled crosses of two parent plant varieties. They are not GMOs.

Mesclun – A mix of assorted young salad greens from lettuces and other greens like mustard, radicchio and arugula.

Mulch – Shredded leaves, compost, chopped bark or any other material which will decay over time, but is spread beneath plants to improve the soil, moderate soil temperature, and retain moisture. Rubber "mulch" does not count.

OMRI-Listed – A product tested and certified by the Organic Materials Review Institute, http://www.omri.org/.

Open Pollinated – Plants that are pollinated by the wind, insects, birds, etc. (See Heirloom Plants.)

Overwinter – To keep plants alive over the winter by bringing them indoors or into a greenhouse.

Perennial – A plant that lives and grows for several consecutive years in place. Some plants are considered hardy perennials because they are tolerant of freezes. Plant hardiness, however, is determined by where the gardener lives. Rosemary may be hardy in some parts of the country and not in others.

Potager – A kitchen garden formally laid out with defined areas. It may contain vegetables, flowers and herbs, but is primarily a kitchen garden, usually located nearby.

Sow – To plant seed. Direct Sow means to plant seeds outdoors directly into the soil in which they will grow.

Three Sisters Planting – Corn, squash and beans planted in concert. Corn first, for structure to support the climbing beans; squash beneath, to shade the others' roots. (Summer melons can be planted in place of squash.) Derived from plantings done by the Iroquois and other Native American tribes.

Thinning – The process of removing some seedlings in order to give others room to grow and produce.

Top Dress – The process of amending the soil by adding a thin layer of fertilizer, like manure, to the surface of the soil.

Zones – Refers to plant hardiness zones in various areas and average ranges of temperatures. See www.planthardiness.ars.usda.gov/

YOUR GARDEN TOOLBOX

LET'S TALK TOOLS. Everyone has a garden toolbox, and everyone's is different. This is mine. As I moved from an urban balcony full of containers to a small suburban yard and then to a larger property, my toolbox changed some, but not as much as you might think.

One of the first things you'll probably need is a hand weeder. You can pull most weeds from containers by hand, but once you move to open beds and borders, you will have more weeds with tougher constitutions. Most weeds come from seeds deposited by birds or are blown in from other locations. You'll also want trowels to transplant seedlings, among other tools. Now you need something to tote your stuff.

Garden tools are just like cutlery and other kitchen tools; although cheap ones work for a while, you'll eventually want to invest in something better. Don't waste your time on plastic garden tools, unless you're doing container gardening. They won't hold up under normal conditions. I buy good kitchen and garden tools because I use them every day. As a result, I rarely have to replace anything. So, while my toolbox isn't cheap, it holds good tools (some of which were received as great gifts).

⇨ **FIVE GALLON BUCKETS** are the best tool for toting in the garden. They are also great to drag behind as I weed.

⇨ **GARDEN BUCKET CADDY.** This type with pockets on the outside of the bucket leaves more room to carry things on the inside, like granular organic fertilizer and larger hand tools.

⇨ **HAND WEEDER.** My favorite is a Dutch hand hoe by DeWit Tools. It comes both left and right handed. CobraHead also makes a great weeder that I use to remove Bermuda grass from sidewalks.

⇨ **GARDEN GLOVES.** Different gloves work for different jobs. Thin Nitrile gloves, cheap and washable, are perfect in the summer and for jobs other than tending prickly roses. I usually don't buy leather gloves because they get dirty and aren't washable. If you can keep yourself from getting dirty while gardening, I'd like to know your secret!

⇨ **BYPASS PRUNERS AND SNIPS.** Even if you only grow vegetables, you'll still need to cut plants back occasionally (like tomatoes). Sharp pruners keep you from breaking your plant. Fiskars PowerGear line of pruners and loppers are my favorites. I also like the super sharp Corona ComfortGEL Floral Snips FS 3204.

⇨ **GARDEN SCISSORS.** If you grow herbs, especially perennial ones, you will need scissors to cut back and deadhead. Fiskars makes good garden scissors.

⇨ **TROWELS.** I like trowels with a thin and sharp edge because they slice through the soil easier. Larger trowels are great for transplanting because they quickly make a perfectly sized hole for a four-inch pot. I have three trowels in my bucket: a Radius Garden ergonomic aluminum hand trowel, a Bond 1906 soil scoop that has a gel grip handle, and a bulb planting trowel.

⇨ **RUBBER COATED PLANT TIES.** It was a happy day when I discovered plant wire that was coated with rubber. It's easy to cut and then bend into shape, and it holds plants gently.

⇨ **PLANT TAGS.** I either buy some at the beginning of the season, or I cut up old mini-blinds and use them for plant tags.

⇨ **SHARPIE OR PAINT PEN.** You always need something to tag your seeds after planting. I promise you won't remember what you planted.

⇨ **WATERING CAN/HOSE AND HOSE END SPRAYER (NOZZLE).** You may also need a small sprayer for manure teas and other organic fungicides and sprays.

⇨ **WATERPROOF NOTEBOOK.** Developed for field studies, Rite in the Rain® spiral notebooks are great for recording when seeds are sown and other observations. An all-weather pen or pencil writes great on them.

Other tools you may need, but aren't on the essential list:

⇨ **HOE.**

⇨ **LEAF RAKE.**

⇨ **SHOVEL OR SPADE.**

⇨ **LAWN MOWER.**

Garden 1

Small Space Gardening
with Containers

Chapter One

Sunshine, Soil and New Beginnings

I'll be showing you how to lay out a container garden, select the right containers for your needs and get started growing some veggies. You'll learn about potting soil, water and seeds and how to decipher a seed packet.

AHH, SPRING. She whispers her siren song on the waft of warm breezes. Tree sap flows, birdsong erupts, and the whole world rejoices in each new leaf. We feel an overwhelming urge to plunge our hands into soil and feel the sun upon our skin. The garden center is crowded with people full of excitement and anticipation. It's intoxicating. We find ourselves piling way too many plants in our baskets. But then comes the tug of panic – so much to choose from, such a small space in which to garden, so little time to devote to it.

Take a deep breath and just be

You don't need a back or front yard to garden. You can garden anywhere. Begin with your balcony or patio. I've gardened wherever I've lived; it didn't matter if it was a mobile home, an apartment or a house with a real back-yard. I guarantee that when you bite into that first sun-ripened tomato or sauté your first homegrown poblano pepper, you will be filled with pride and joy. On top of that, your friends will be amazed. Trust me.

Although this chapter is about your first year of gardening, go ahead and skip ahead through the following chapters as you need to, or as the mood strikes you. You may have an outbreak of insects or disease before I can teach you about that, or perhaps you want to grow fruit, and this chapter doesn't talk much about fruit. There's no "right" way to progress with a garden, or with this book. Things come up. I have some favorite garden books that I enjoy reading cover to cover just for the pleasure of it. Maybe you'll want to do that, too, before you ever open your first bag of potting mix.

First things

START SMALL

When I was a little girl, my family often ate at a local cafeteria where I always chose more food than I could eat. My dad teased me, saying my eyes were bigger than my stomach. Going too large in a garden is like overfilling your plate. Only plan for the number of pots you can easily water. Before you buy six packages of lettuce seed, remember that you don't need to grow everything you eat. Give yourself permission to buy the rest from local farmers, a CSA (Community Supported Agriculture), or the organic section of the grocery store. Although there is something special about pulling an onion straight from the dirt or snipping herbs just before dinner, nothing is more soul sapping than a too-large garden gone bad midsummer. Depending upon your watering system and space limitations, you can replicate all eight containers in this chapter's plan, or narrow it down to three for the first year. You can even start with one. It's your garden. No garden police will check on your progress.

Your site

Starting a garden is like taking a college course or beginning a new job. Before you head to the nursery, read through the entire plan and ask yourself some questions.

~ What do I like to eat?
~ Where will I place my containers?
~ Will my plants be on an uncovered patio, deck or balcony?
~ Do I have access to water?

Patios, decks and balconies all have similar but unique conditions. Apartment balconies may not be able to support heavier containers, so it's best to use lightweight pots whenever possible (you may also not like moving heavy containers full of soil). Situate heavier items closer to the building along load-bearing supports. It's a good idea to check your lease to make sure you abide by any restrictions.

There's always room for a garden, even if you don't think you have enough space. Look for a sunny place that's not being used. I've seen driveways, roofs and other unlikely spaces with containers full of food plants and flowers.

BALCONY GARDEN

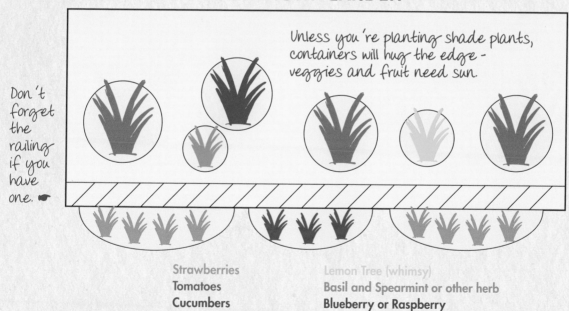

Unless you're planting shade plants, containers will hug the edge - veggies and fruit need sun.

Don't forget the railing if you have one. ☞

Strawberries
Tomatoes
Cucumbers

Lemon Tree (whimsy)
Basil and Spearmint or other herb
Blueberry or Raspberry

DECK OR PATIO GARDEN

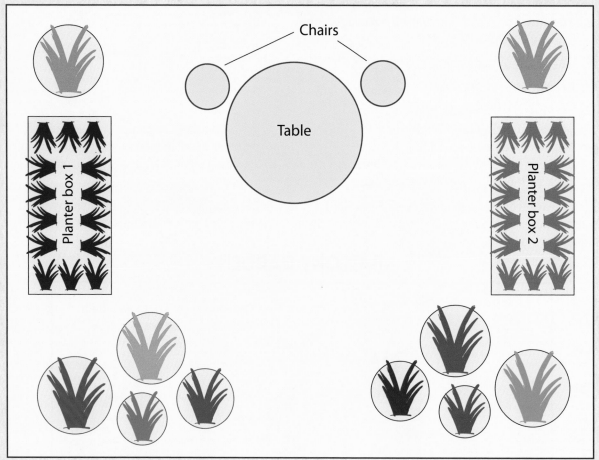

Chairs

Table

Planter box 1

Planter box 2

SPRING

Strawberries	Spring Onions
Lettuce & Spinach	Pansies
Chives - Perennial	Radishes
Swiss Chard	Nasturtium

SUMMER

Tomatoes in Planter box 2
Squash
Eggplant or trellised Zucchini in Planter box 1
Cucumbers
Green Beans (pole type, trellised)
Radishes and Swiss Chard *– trade out to peppers – either hot or sweet*

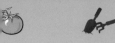

Here comes the sun

Most vegetables, being sun worshippers, need at least six hours of natural light each day to perform their best. If your patio faces east, where the sun rises, I have wonderful news: east means morning sun and maybe even all-day sunshine, depending on how far from your house or building the pots are placed.

A west or south-facing area will be much hotter, getting afternoon or all-day sun. If your area faces north, you'll have cooler temperatures and more shade. That isn't a bad thing if you live in a hot climate, but in cool, rainy places like Portland or Seattle you'll need all the sunshine you can find.

The sun becomes much stronger as summer progresses and the sun's angle changes. In hot climates, morning sun is always best for your plants, but with a little ingenuity and some shade cloth (see page 80), you can grow in afternoon sun as well.

Pots don't have to just sit there

You can move them around as needs or whims arise. Don't have enough sun? Want to change the look of your garden space? Here's one of the great things about container gardens: they're mobile.

Tools of the Trade

Containers should be at least 18 to 24 inches wide and 12 to 16 inches deep to provide plenty of room for your plants. One benefit to using larger containers is they don't dry out as quickly as smaller ones. Small pots can look nice tucked into small spaces, though. It helps if you line porous containers with some type of material that retains water. I sometimes use a layer of sphagnum moss in mine around the edges, but I have also used bubble wrap. I like moss better because it's natural.

There are several different kinds of containers to choose from. Here's what you need to know to pick the best ones for your garden:

⇨ **TERRA COTTA.** Terra cotta is porous, so it heats up quickly and drains rapidly. In a hot climate, it can dry out too quickly. However, it is wonderful for large, top-heavy plants that need a sturdy pot.

⇨ **PLASTIC.** Don't belittle the humble plastic container. While it might not be the sportiest one on the block, it will get you through your first and probably second season just fine. Plastics with bisphenol A (BPA) have been in the news recently because of their potential link to cancer. There is debate about whether you should choose BPA-free plastic to grow vegetables. BPA is understandably controversial, and research is ongoing. For my own garden, I use organic practices throughout; last year I chose food-grade plastic buckets to grow my potatoes. There's still scientific discussion about whether BPA leaches into growing vegetables. That's not to say that it doesn't, though. To be safe, I would choose food-grade plastic or a completely different type of container to grow fruit and vegetables, just in case.

⇨ **INSULATED CONTAINERS.** These are an excellent medium for flowers. However, since they are not made of food-grade plastic, I wouldn't use them to grow anything I'd want to eat. They also hold moisture – not ideal in rainy climates, but can be very beneficial in dry climates.

⇨ **GLAZED CERAMIC CONTAINERS.** Glazed containers are a good choice because the glazing retains moisture. But, they are heavy and can crack like terra cotta if left outside over winter. Glazed containers can also be pricey, so it's best to collect them a few at a time. I grow most of my plants in cobalt blue glazed pots I've gathered over the years.

⇨ **CONCRETE AND HYPERTUFA.** These are additional container choices. Minerals that bleed out of concrete tend to make soil more alkaline. I've never had problems with this, but if you grow a crop like blueberries you will probably need to add sulphur to acidify the soil.

⇨ **METAL CONTAINERS.** For sheer modern, architectural style, nothing beats the silvery goodness and contemporary charm of galvanized steel stock tanks, or other lead-free, metal containers. They make great small ponds, too.

⇨ **UPCYCLED ITEMS.** I've seen plants grown in everything from bathtubs to plastic storage bins. Use your imagination to create a garden that's practically free!

Container selections are nearly endless. Whatever type you pick, it's good to be aware of the pluses and minuses of each material before you choose.

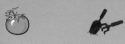

Drainage holes and saucers

All containers need drainage holes. Containers do not need saucers; they trap water and debris and are no longer suggested. If you want to lift your pot off of a deck or patio, use pot feet or a pot trivet. I also use small, flat rocks to level my containers and improve drainage.

What size container?

Container size is important, too. It must be large enough to accommodate the plant's roots. Tomatoes and peppers especially need large containers. Although they aren't fancy, five-gallon buckets are excellent choices for large plants. Be sure to drill those drainage holes first, though.

> **TIP:** Most plants also need good air circulation, so try not to overcrowd them. Keep in mind how large they will eventually grow, and leave a little space around the containers themselves, too. Gentle breezes keep foliage dry and disease free. However, try to keep containers out of strong winds that dry out soil and shred leaves.

Potting soil (it's not dirt)

Who says you need dirt to garden? Good quality potting mixes can be found at your local nursery. Don't be surprised to see the words "soilless mix" on a package. Most potting soils are mixtures of several ingredients. Many start with peat moss, which can be controversial due to the environmental damage of peat bogs. For more regarding peat bogs and their environmental impact on wetlands, see Resources. Don't be afraid to ask your local nursery what goes into their soil mix. It should be organic. You're growing these vegetables partly because you don't completely trust commercial farming, right? Don't grow with chemical fertilizers or pesticides either, and the ecosystem will thank you.

Garden soil. This is a no-go for pots because it is too heavy, slow draining and has weed seeds and bacteria. Container mixes are formulated to be light in texture, free of disease and weed seeds, and to provide good drainage.

Water: the stuff of life

So, you've picked your pots, plants and soil, and you're ready to go. However, without water, your garden will quickly become a barren wasteland. All life needs water to survive. Plants should be placed where they are easy for you to water. Many apartments don't have an outside water spigot on the balcony. If that's the case, either hook up a hose to your kitchen faucet – with a faucet adapter – or carry water to your plants. Your choice comes down to convenience. If you plan to tote water to your plants, buy a good quality watering can. Plastic watering cans are lightweight and easy to carry, even when full of water. I particularly love Haws watering cans – a good Christmas present – because they are perfectly balanced, with a great watering rose (sprinkler).

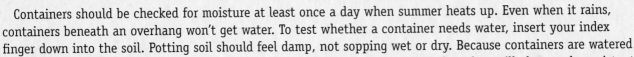

Containers should be checked for moisture at least once a day when summer heats up. Even when it rains, containers beneath an overhang won't get water. To test whether a container needs water, insert your index finger down into the soil. Potting soil should feel damp, not sopping wet or dry. Because containers are watered

everyday, they will also need consistent nutrients. Buy a slow release or water-soluble organic fertilizer for monthly feeding. Group containers together for easier watering on hot summer days. You will probably water your plants before you head off to work, and no one wants to haul a hose around the deck while wearing office attire.

Drip watering. For even sweeter relief, install a drip watering system with a timer. This is perfect for when you leave town because containers can become diseased or die if they go more than a day or two without water. You can buy kits and additional drip emitters at varying water rates, all very easy to install. I placed a simple timer on mine to make sure the pots got watered to my specifications while I was gone. (See the next chapter for how to install a drip system for your pots.) If possible, group your containers together in the shade to reduce water loss. Have a veggie-loving friend come over to pick vegetables and check on things while you're away. Some vegetables will quit producing if you leave them alone for too long.

Good to know: Crops like lettuce and other leafy vegetables require more water than bulbs like onions and garlic.

Project Salad Bowl

What you'll need:

○ A shallow bowl-shaped planter
○ Two varieties of lettuce seed or a mesclun mix of seeds
○ Potting soil
○ Watering can
○ Your two hands

When I saw this terra-cotta-colored, plastic planter at my local home improvement center, I just knew I had to make a salad bowl.

If your container doesn't have holes, take a hammer and screwdriver, or an electric drill, and make five or six holes spaced throughout the bottom of the container. This is to help it drain properly. If the container is pottery, you'll need a masonry drill bit.

Place soil in the container until it's about 1/2 inch from the top.

From this point, you can do it one of two ways:

I decided to plant mine in a swirl pattern so I dragged a bamboo spatula through the soil. You could also use play sand to mark your design. I then sowed seeds along the swirl pattern.

If you don't want to go to this much trouble, scatter the mixed seeds of a mesclun mix over the top of the soil. Lightly cover them with soil. Seeds will usually sprout in 7 to 10 days, but check your seed package for germination dates.

Water soil and keep it evenly moist, but don't drown seeds with too much water either. Place the bowl outside, but keep it elevated to prevent rot on your deck and bunnies eating all of your salad.

When plants get to the desired size, you can either cut them like mesclun, or let them grow to maturity. I know it's hard to wait!

TIP: If you have large enough containers, you can interplant shorter or trailing plants with taller ones like tomatoes, for extra visual appeal. Even add some flowers. (This squash plant looks lonely!)

Seeds or plants? Which are better?

It all depends upon the plant and your point of view. There are some people who think seeds are the only way to garden, but some plants, like tomatoes and peppers, take a while to grow before they begin producing fruit. While I do start heirloom tomato seeds indoors, I also buy some hybrid plants from my local nursery. You're a gardener the moment your hands touch the soil, even if you only buy plants.

What to grow?

Grow what you love to eat. Radishes may be quick and easy, but if you don't like them, why waste the space? In my family, we like lettuce, spinach, spring onions, tomatoes, cucumbers, squash, okra and corn. All of these, except for okra and corn, can easily be grown in containers. Before heading to the nursery, make a list of those vegetables you love to eat and grow those first. If you have a hankering to try something new, go for it, too. A few years ago, my daughter, Claire, and I discovered we love kale chips, especially homemade ones. The kale we found in the grocery store was large and tough. We began growing 'Toscano' or dinosaur kale, and we now have some in raised beds during the cool seasons. Kale, like lettuce, chard and spinach, is easy to grow in containers, and using seed for these leafy crops works well. You can also buy plants if you want to jumpstart the season. We sow kale in late fall, and it often overwinters in our warm climate with cover. We also do an early spring sowing in February.

What about hanging baskets?

Use hanging baskets for trailing plants like strawberries (three plants per basket), along with certain cherry tomatoes like 'Red Robin' and 'Losetto.' You can even grow runner beans and trailing squash in hanging baskets; their stems will trail down the sides. Fair warning: I wasn't successful with those trendy containers that grew tomatoes upside down. You might have better luck.

   In a hot climate, hanging baskets dry out faster than containers on the ground, so choose those that are solid or are lined with actual moss, not coir. If hanging baskets dry out, your plants will be stunted and may not fruit well.

Deciphering a Seed Packet
(what does all this stuff mean?)

Some seed companies give you more information than others. Two of the best packets on the market are those from Botanical Interests and Renee's Garden. Both companies offer great seeds, too. Each approaches the seed packet a bit differently, though. Here's BI's approach.

FRONT:

At the top of the package is the plant's common name: LETTUCE Leaf. Right away, you know you're growing a romaine or butterhead type of lettuce. Below that is the cultivar or selection name, 'Red Sails.' And then the botanical name, *Lactuca sativa,* not necessary but it certainly doesn't hurt, either. Read your seed packets, and before long, Latin will be tripping off your tongue. Just kidding. Still, when you grow flowers and ornamental plants, botanical names are very helpful.

> LETTUCE LEAF
> *Red Sails*
> *Lactuca sativa*
>
> $1.89
> 750 mg
>
> **COOL SEASON**
> **45 DAYS**
> Sow in early spring through fall
>
> *This fancy buttery lettuce with ruffled burgundy tinged leaves is a salad lover's dream. 1985 All America Selections winner. Very heat tolerant, grow all summer!*
>
> *Botanical*
> INTERESTS®

What else you'll see on the front:

At left is the price: $1.89

Amount of seed in the package by weight: 750 mg

Whether the plant is warm or cool season: cool

How many days until maturity: 45

When to sow seed: Early spring through fall. This is where things get tricky. You may be able to do that in New England, but not in the middle south where I live. We get two seasons of lettuce, and that's all. Even though this information is helpful, always refer to the USDA Zone map online at www.planthardiness.ars.usda.gov/ and your local Cooperative Extension Office for exactly when you can sow certain seeds.

Description of the plant: Here you learn 'Red Sails' is a 1985 All America Selection and that it's very heat tolerant. Awesome.

There is also a lovely drawing of what the plant should look like, by Donna Clement. I like photographs or drawings, but drawings are a bit more romantic, aren't they?

11

BACK:

On the left is a tag you can cut out to attach to a wooden plant stake for I.D., if you like. If you do, cover it with adhesive, waterproof tape. I tend to use plastic markers instead and just write the variety on them; partly because I rarely use the entire package of seeds in one go. However, on this tag, BI lists all kinds of pertinent information like how deep to sow the seeds and when to thin them. They even tell you how far apart to thin your tiny plants.

On the right side, they explain how 'Red Sails' grows and that it makes a great patio container variety. This package will plant eight 10-foot rows. That's a whole lotta lettuce. Note, most people don't use the entire package, and if they do, lettuce seeds are very small. You usually have to thin them when direct sown. So, unless you use a small-seed planter, like a dial seed sower, you probably won't get eight 10-foot rows. I think there are better things to do in life than worry about spacing tiny lettuce seeds, but that's just me.

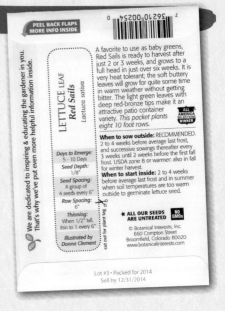

Below this information, they tell you it is recommended to sow 'Red Sails' seeds directly outdoors. Plants often have a preference about how they want to be sown. Some like indoors, or they take too long to grow in one season unless you start them early. On the bottom of the packet you see the sell-by date and when the seed was packed. Don't stop there, either. Inside the packet is more information about your lettuce.

Check out Renee's seeds, too. And the grandfather of seed companies, Burpee, whose seed packets give all their information in English and Spanish. They also include a zone map showing when plants should be grown in your area.

Confession: It took me a very long time to attempt seeds. I think I feared failure. Don't let nerves stop you from growing plants from seed. It can be very rewarding to grow an entire plant from something no bigger than a grain of rice. I wish I had possessed the courage to start sooner!

* * *

Way to go!

By combining these tools and techniques from year one, you should be on your way to having yourself a real, live, potted vegetable garden, even if it's one or two plants. Congratulations – you're a gardener now!

Chapter Two

Three Seasons of Plenty: Spring, Summer and Fall

This is where you learn how to extend your container garden's growing season well into fall; how to start seeds indoors; how to increase diversity with veggies and herbs, and how to rotate your container crops... and how to prepare your container garden for its winter sleep.

HOW WAS YOUR FIRST GROWING SEASON? What were your successes? Did some plants just "up and die?" I know it's hard, but try to concentrate more on success than failure. We tend to focus on the things we don't do well, but let those go. Successful gardeners know that some years, no matter what we do, we are unable to grow much. Other years are full of bounty. We learn to go with the flow.

Each new garden year starts with a review:

~ How did your containers perform last year?

~ Did your vegetables get enough sun, or too much?

~ Do your pots need to be moved to a sunnier location?

~ Should you buy a bit of shade cloth before the hot summer sun wilts your flowers and veggies? (See page 80 for shade cloth information.)

~ Which plants had problems with bugs or disease?

Success inspires adventure in the garden. Even in the depths of winter, gardeners can hold onto this excitement by studying up on something they want to try next year. It keeps us young. Not that you need to be concerned yet, but gardeners are the "youngest" people I know.

About the danger of seed catalogs.

Gardening season starts early. By mid-January, seed catalogs begin to arrive in your snail-mailbox, along with links to online catalogs in your email. Beware the danger of jumping in with both feet. Seed catalogs are a terrible temptation for the winter-weary gardener. Before you place your order, look at your notes for those vegetables you loved last year.

Once you've got an idea of what to order, go ahead and try something new. How about an heirloom lettuce? All leafy greens grow well in containers – lettuces, spinach, kale, chard, and mesclun (a mix of different lettuce seeds and other leafy greens). So do spring onions when you buy them as onion sets (small bulbs). Onions seeds work too, but they'll take a lot longer. Beets, carrots and turnips are root crops that thrive in containers. While it's good to make sure you don't go crazy when ordering seeds, dare yourself to experiment with something new. It could become your favorite veggie or fruit.

TIP: With the help of Siri on my iPhone, I keep notes throughout the garden season. This info syncs with my laptop and makes my job easier in January, when I'm tempted to order too much, too soon. I do my best thinking when I am in the garden, so it's great to capture those thoughts for later use.

Getting the jump on spring

Containers have an advantage with early spring crops: the soil inside a container warms up earlier than the soil in the ground, and stays warm because the container will hold in heat. That gives your container plants a head start. You can often produce two series of leafy greens before summer. I am especially enamored with lettuces. I have such a short season to grow them, but nothing beats the taste of fresh lettuce with a light olive oil vinaigrette. I love 'Nevada,' 'Speckled Troutback' and 'Black-seeded Simpson', among others. I always include a spicy mesclun mix in my spring garden, as well. It wakes up my palate after a long winter of eating soups and other warming but heavy foods.

Sometimes, I plant loads of new varieties, but if you're short on container space and you have some actual ground to work with as well, you'll want to curb your enthusiasm until we get to Garden Two; that's where you'll have more room to play in the dirt.

Starting Seeds Indoors

You may already realize that in order to grow what you want, you are going to need to start some of your seeds indoors. I can sow lettuce outside in late February for a spring crop, but if I want a fall crop of tender leaves for my salad bowl, I must start them inside, because my summer weather is too hot for lettuce to germinate outside. You may not have this problem.

Don't stress...let me lead you through the process. Here's what you'll need.

⇨ **CONTAINERS.** Some type of seed-starting container. These can be traditional six-pack cells that fit into a flat, or they can be almost anything. Throughout the year, I collect small, plastic containers to upcycle for indoor seed starting. There's no need to buy special items and trays unless you want them. I especially like sour cream tubs and plastic to-go containers from my local Pei Wei Asian Diner. They are the perfect size, and they have covers to keep moisture in for the first few days. Be sure to punch holes in the bottom for drainage. Smaller cells, like six packs, warm up faster, but seedlings will need to be transplanted sooner. Simple broadcast sowing into these containers works well with most plants if you don't mind pricking the roots gently apart and transplanting into larger containers later. This is my preferred sowing method now.

TIP: Saving fast food and other containers is a good way to reuse items bound for the landfill. Winter may be heading our way almost as we harvest the summer veggies, but indoor seed sowing for spring begins again right after Christmas when those catalogs arrive in our mail boxes again.

⇨ **GRIT,** any type. I use chicken grit sold at feed stores to top off my seed trays. It helps them to retain water and keeps seeds from shifting due to overhead watering. It's not absolutely necessary, but I like it.

⇨ **COVER.** If you don't have lids to fit your seed starting containers, use plastic wrap. I like Press'n Seal® myself, because you can attach it to the sides of the container. It isn't organic, but it doesn't touch your plants either. You remove it as soon as seeds are up and growing with two sets of leaves. Insert little vertical plant tags into the soil to keep plastic wrap off of your seedlings.

⇨ **POTTING SOIL.** Potting soil. Special seed-starting soil is sold with seed packs. However, as long as your potting soil is rich in nutrients, well-drained and organic, you can use most potting soil. I find that the seed-starting soils tend to bubble up if I water them from above, and sometimes, it disturbs my seeds. One way to prevent this is to water from below, by placing an inch or so of water in a tray and setting your containers inside it. Once the soil in your containers looks damp on top, dump out the water. Either way works. Make sure your potting soil is damp, but not soaking wet, before you start.

⇨ **SEEDS.**

⇨ **PLANT TAGS AND A SHARPIE.** You simply must write down what you've planted because in the rush of getting things into the ground, you won't remember which plant is which.

⇨ **A LIGHT SOURCE.** Buying lights for seed starting can be as complicated as writing about compost, or as simple. Seeds can be started in a sunny window, but I found mine performed better and grew faster if they had additional light. I started with two sets of full-spectrum fluorescent lights that I mounted beneath the windowsills in our living room. I still use these once plants are growing, and I want to start more seeds elsewhere. Plants get the natural light from the window along with that of your light source.

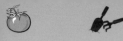

Once I had grown a few things from seed, I had the seed-starting bug! I built myself a seed-starting station, and it's located in the dining room next to the kitchen, where it's easy for me to remember to water. It's a simple one-two-three thing to set up. (See how on the following page.)

⇨ **HEAT MATS.** Many seeds benefit from heat from below. I've listed my source for heat mats in the Resources section at the back of the book.

What to sow?

That's easy: sow veggies you crave. Always be open to new vegetables, but don't plant an entire flat of arugula unless you love it.

In warm climates like mine, you can sow seed in late summer for vegetables like kale, chard and lettuce that don't germinate so well in hot weather. I always sow a flat or two of these yummy veggies to harvest outside in fall.

Build a seed-starting station

To build a seed-starting station, you'll need the following:

○ **Metal Rack,** with adjustable shelves because as plants grow, you will need to move the light source further away. You can also put lights on adjustable chains if you can't find a rack with shelves that move. Knowing my tendency to go big, I bought a five-foot tall metal closet rack. A shorter one would be fine, but I wouldn't go taller. This one stretches nearly to my dining room ceiling.

○ **Four Casters** to make your seed station easy to move. Mine stays in the dining room near the kitchen where there is water. My potting bench, a./k./a., kitchen sink, is one door away. That's also where I write so I spend time there everyday. We have a basement, but I'm a forgetful plant mama.

○ **Four-foot light fixtures** with full-spectrum, fluorescent bulbs. Note: Fixtures must be grounded, attached to the metal frame and then plugged into a grounded wall fixture to prevent electric shock.

○ **Four large heat mats,** or eight smaller ones. Once plants are up and growing, you will no longer need heat mats unless your house is cold. These must also be plugged into a grounded wall fixture.

○ **Seed trays** or other containers. If you use recycled trays and inserts, first dunk them in a ten percent, bleach solution to clean them and remove bacteria.

○ **Seeds**

- **Soilless seed starting mix** or other potting mix. Don't try to reuse your potting soil from previous containers as seedlings are highly susceptible to bacteria; and

- **A watering can** or a nearby water faucet. For the first few days, when seeds are covered by plastic, a watering can is great. Later, thirsty plants benefit from soaking in trays of water for a short time. I sometimes use jelly roll pans or cookie sheets with raised sides to soak trays from the bottom. You could also use rubber containers, a kitchen sink, or a bathtub to soak trays.

Assemble the metal rack. I chose metal because water won't damage the finish. Wood wouldn't work well in this situation. Attach the lights either with adjustable chains or metal flanges. We like chains best. Insert light bulbs. You will need to stick them into the fixture and usually give a slight turn to lock them in place. Plug lights and warming mats into a grounded electrical outlet. It must be grounded because water and electricity mixed together is shocking and dangerous. Mine are plugged into a grounded power strip. Place heating mats below lights, and your seed starting station is open and ready for business.

How do I know what seeds to buy? (food preferences and food limitations)

I thought I knew what I liked to eat, but after being diagnosed gluten and dairy (casein) intolerant in 2007, I discovered a whole new world of food. Gone were whole wheat breads and fluffy pastries, but in their place, I stumbled upon Thai and Hispanic cuisines. They became the backbone of my diet. For me, suddenly, there was a wide, new world of chiles, Asian eggplant, quinoa, rice – brown or Jasmine – basils, onions, garlic, etc.

I don't limit myself to restaurant eating, either. I now grow more chile peppers – four hot and three mild this year – three varieties of garlic, onions/shallots, three kinds of basil, including Thai and Italian types, and tomatoes. An entire chapter could be devoted to tomatoes. There are so many from which to choose. Asian cuisine is held up by the mighty rice grain, while Mexican and other Latino foods are often based upon corn. I buy organic cornmeal, but I also grow sweet corn that is open-pollinated (see the Glossary), organic and not genetically modified (GMO).

Rice isn't local to Oklahoma, but a lot of it grows in Texas, Arkansas and Louisiana. Occasionally, I head to an Asian grocery store in the city to buy fresh rice, but not often. Food controls in China aren't all that I wish they were. I also worry about arsenic levels in rice, so I balance my favorite grain with loads of other vegetables.

Perhaps, you'll have a little brown rice left over from dinner and want some fried with vegetables for lunch.

Then, you'll want to grow Thai basil so that you always have it fresh right outside your door. Basil is an aromatic herb and doesn't keep well. It's also pricey at the store and very easy to grow, spring to fall. So, if nothing else, plant basil and other herbs.

Herbs I grow:

⇨ **ROSEMARY:** perennial in my climate. It needs very sharp drainage.

⇨ **BASIL:** 'Sweet Genovese,' 'Siam Queen,' 'Spicy Bush (a tiny one for containers) and 'Purple Ruffles' (an attractive variety that makes beautiful basil vinegar in summer).

⇨ **DILL:** 'Leafy Diana' is an heirloom variety that is small, compact and beautiful.

⇨ **SAGE:** Common garden sage, *Salvia officinalis,* and 'Aurea', a golden variety that stays small.

⇨ **THYME:** Common thyme, *Thymus vulgaris,* along with lemon thyme.

⇨ **PARSLEY, ITALIAN:** flat-leafed; more tasty than the curly type.

Excluding thyme, sage and rosemary, I direct sow all of the above as seeds, but to get a jump on the season, I often buy an extra plant from the nursery, or I start one variety of an herb indoors. I always grow extra dill and flat-leafed parsley for the caterpillars. I love my butterflies.

I make a mean Thai basil eggplant and a wonderful Thai fried rice in a variety of combinations. Once you understand the basics of a cuisine, it's easy to tweak it to your preferences. I'm telling you this because you may find Italian food your favorite. If so, you'll want to grow 'San Marzano' tomatoes, beautiful onions, garlic, basil, perhaps oregano, thyme, eggplant and Italian parsley.

Know your favorite cuisine, and you can replicate your favorite flavors even without takeout.

When and how do I start?

For a spring garden, generally start seeds approximately eight weeks before your last expected spring frost date. To find that date, contact your local cooperative extension office. Plant seedlings outdoors two weeks after your last frost date.

Seeds love moist soil, so wet your potting mix first to where it clings together, but isn't soaked. Moisture helps seeds shed their seed coat and start growing. That's why you'll read articles about soaking seed before sowing. Certain seeds, like morning glories and okra, benefit from being soaked 24 hours before planting. You can also nick these seeds with a small knife if you're impatient to sow and forgot to soak them.

Smaller seeds, like lettuce seeds, don't need much soil to cover. Larger seeds will need to be a deeper planting. Don't worry too much about planting depth. The average seed-starting container is no more than three inches. Plants will find their way to the top. Do read seed packets though for specific information because some seeds need light to germinate.

Check seeds daily to make sure they aren't drying out. Soil should be moist, but not soaked. Seed trays dry out quickly. Once seeds germinate, take off the plastic or cover and place trays back under the lights. Be aware that once you remove the plastic covers, soil dries out more quickly. Don't let your little seedlings founder.

Moving day

Once plants are two to three inches tall and have two or three sets of leaves, I select the strongest plants and transplant them into larger containers, usually four-inch pots.

Fill four-inch pots with potting soil. Gently turn over the original container into the palm of your hand, and soil will usually come loose, but you can squeeze the bottom of the container if necessary. With your fingers, lift your babies from their container. Look for white roots against the dark soil and move plants gently apart from each other trying not to disturb the roots too much.

With a stick or your finger, make an indentation into the new container and place the seedling inside. Firm the soil around the base of the plant and straighten it in its new home.

Tomato and pepper plants are very forgiving of this process. You can even place soil up to just below their top leaves. They will form roots along their stems. This process of "pricking out" shocks the young plants, so gently water them and begin feeding with diluted liquid fertilizer, like manure tea (see page 77 for how to make your own). Although they may look shocked for a bit, they'll come around if you feed and water them. Give them good light and remember to turn their pots frequently so that they grow straight and tall.

While you can start seeds in a window that gets good light, like a south-facing one, I found I had better luck with additional lighting. My first seeds were grown on stone ledges in our living room with lights inserted beneath our windowsills. I didn't grow much there, but I did have success.

My plants are growing. Now what?

This is a good thing! As your plants grow, outdoor weather will begin to settle down. Continue to water and feed seedlings. When weather warms, take your small plants outdoors to harden them off before transplanting outside. Hardening off is the process of introducing your tender plants to the wild. Start taking them outside on a mild day and let them stay out for an hour or so, increasing the time over the next week or two. In the

beginning, I wasn't good at hardening off because I left my plants in the sun. Living in the South, I've learned you need to place plants in shade first, and later in the process, partial shade. I also set my kitchen timer or smartphone timer, to remind me to bring them back indoors. You are teaching your small plants how to live with less babying, while enduring stronger light, wind and other outdoor issues. Protect them from strong winds, too – and place plants where your dogs or cats won't knock them over. I've gone outside to find my plants dumped over and dead, and yes, I sat down and cried.

After plants are hardened off, it's time to transplant them to their permanent home. This can be an even larger container – at least 18 inches – or into a raised bed, or the ground. Where you place your seedlings will depend upon your garden size and location.

Let's get growing.

Spring

Check your local cooperative extension service or independent nursery for a chart or map with last freeze and first frost dates in your region. Base your planning on it, but keep an eye on the weather. Sometimes Mother Nature fools us especially in spring. If you see a hard freeze – below 32°F – in the forecast, move pots closer to your home and cover them. Most early spring vegetables can handle frost, but not a hard freeze. Containers are also more open to the weather because their soil is elevated.

TIP: You can grow potatoes in five-gallon buckets. To get more potatoes per plant, gradually cover the potato starts with soil as they grow. Also, provide regular watering for continued growth and well-drained soil to prevent rot.

Potting Mixes. Replace or not? That's a good question.

You may read elsewhere to replace your potting soil each year, to prevent a buildup of disease. Well, I don't replace mine every year. I remove the top third of the potting soil for those containers I replant with annual flowers or vegetables. By the time I pull out the previous seasons' dead plants, much of the soil comes away from the pot with the roots. I comb my hands through what is left and then replace the missing soil with new potting mix and a dose of natural (not chemical) fertilizer. For containers with long-term shrubs, like blueberries, raspberries or roses, I top off last year's soil with compost and a touch of organic granular fertilizer.

To replace potting soil each year wouldn't be cost effective or even environmentally responsible. Plus, can you imagine the work to carry bags of soil into an apartment or condominium every year? No thanks.

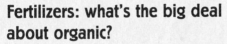

Fertilizers: what's the big deal about organic?

When you walk into the garden center you'll probably see brightly colored containers of fertilizer next to the plants you want to buy. That's done on purpose. The makers of both chemical fertilizers and chemical controls, along with organic producers, now package everything according to what you're growing. You can choose to buy fertilizer in a bright red package, specially formulated for tomatoes if you want, but I suggest you look over the ingredients on the back first. Most organic fertilizers work for most vegetables and fruits. I use an all-purpose, granulated fertilizer for most of my plants. Many retail, organic fertilizers are made from poultry yards. Check the back of the package where ingredients are listed to see where ingredients are sourced from.

Recently, there's been valid concern about animal manures and compost damaging and killing plants due to persistent herbicides. These herbicides are used by some farmers and ranchers to kill selected weeds in their fields. They are a chemical control, and studies have shown they remain in an animal's manure even after being digested. Regular composting won't degrade them either. This means if you use a manure or compost with persistent herbicides, your seeds may not germinate, or your plants won't thrive. They may even die. We're at a crossroads in gardening and agriculture where we need to know how composts are made and which farm produced the manure. Don't be afraid to ask questions, whether you get compost locally or buy from a national manufacturer.

Even with good potting mix, you will need fertilizer for some plants. Containers leach nutrients when they are watered daily in summer (in hot climates, twice a day).

There are many options on the market. I simply buy one that has molasses and seaweed in it, along with fish emulsion (poop). Drenching your plants with organic fertilizer is like giving them a vitamin boost. Some of these fertilizers can be quite smelly for a day or two so consider the ingredients before buying. While you can use

TIP: Leaf lettuces are among the easiest to grow because they sprout quickly and can be eaten early within a few weeks.

TIP: **Initial setup.** Use organic compost on top of the potting mix, as both a mulch and a balanced fertilizer. I also mix in granular, organic fertilizer at the time of planting. Once summer heat begins to build, and I'm watering daily, I drench hungry plants every other week with an organic liquid fertilizer I mix with water. I've used prepackaged manure teas like the ones listed in Resources, and I've made my own smelly mix (see my smelly recipe on page 77).

chemical fertilizers, I wouldn't. One of the reasons we garden at home is to ease the chemical load in our food supply. Using chemical fertilizers defeats this purpose. Also, organic fertilizers contain trace elements and microorganisms chemical fertilizers don't have.

What do the initials NPK mean?

When I first began gardening, I read a lot of information about nitrogen (N), phosphorous (P) and potassium (K), and honestly, my eyes glazed over. I'm not a chemist, and I like to think of gardening as more of a creative endeavor, but here's a quick explanation of those NPK numbers you'll find listed on fertilizer packages.

⇨ **NITROGEN** makes leaves grow. Plants with sufficient nitrogen are healthy, growing and green. A lack of nitrogen is called chlorosis and is shown in sad, yellowing leaves. Chlorosis should not be confused with chartreuse plants like 'Black Seeded Simpson' lettuce, which is naturally a lovely light green.

⇨ **PHOSPHORUS** is synonymous with healthy flowers and root systems.

⇨ **POTASSIUM,** i.e., potash, is needed for plant development and general well being.

Healthy soil also needs trace elements and microorganisms, which are replenished with compost (and not through chemical fertilizers).

Overusing fertilizers, especially chemical ones, on lawns and gardens leaches excess nitrogen, phosphorus and potassium into our streams, lakes and rivers. This increases algae bloom and pollution. Something to consider.

So, now you're probably thinking that adding a high nitrogen fertilizer to your plants is a great idea ("makes leaves grow"). No, it's not. Too much nitrogen will cause your plants to *overgrow* and attract insects. If you want more aphids and other beasties troubling your plants, give them an extra dose of nitrogen. Once, and only once, my husband and I added fresh chicken manure to our vegetable garden in spring, thinking it was a good idea. It wasn't. Chicken manure is extremely "hot," meaning it has excessive nitrogen until it ages for six months or so. I now add composted chicken manure to my main vegetable garden at the end of the growing season so it breaks down and becomes part of the soil. Composting makes all the difference.

The NPK numbers game. Don't go number crazy, either. You may be tempted to use chemical fertilizers because they boast higher number ratios than organic fertilizers, whose numbers tend to be low. Instead, look to the health of your plants. Adding a good quality, organic granular fertilizer to the potting mix at the time of planting will get most of your vegetables through the season. Heavy feeders, like indeterminate tomatoes, may need a boost midsummer. (Note: *Indeterminate* refers to varieties of tomatoes that keep growing larger and taller, and produce fruit through the whole season.)

Crop rotation, pot-style

Crop rotation was another term that drove me nuts. It sounds so agricultural college, but it's merely moving your crops each year to defeat disease and other problems. Some vegetables also require more "food" than others. Certain plants, like tomatoes and corn, are greedy, while beans, peas, and other legumes add nitrogen back to the soil. If you grew a tomato or a squash in a pot this year, try bush or pole green beans there next time. If you plant pole beans, place a structure for support in the pot.

One of the great thing about containers is you have so much choice and can easily try new things.

Summer

Choosing summer cultivars is simpler than you may think.

Add tomatoes and other heat lovers beginning in late April or early May. Depending upon your climate, you may want to even wait until June. Again, consult your local cooperative extension service for dates. In my climate, tomatoes, green beans, eggplant, sweet potatoes, peppers and heat-loving herbs like basil really strut their stuff once cold weather crops are nearly finished.

TIP: When lettuce tastes bitter and starts to elongate into flower, I save a plant or two and let them bloom. Why do that? Pollinators seem especially attracted to simple flowers like those of vegetables, and I'm always trying to encourage pollination in my garden.

In the South, it's a good idea to start tomatoes indoors or buy plants soon enough to have them fruiting before temperatures rise to over 100°F or blooms won't set and become fruit. Blossom drop happens when temperatures rise over 100°F and is an early frustration for new gardeners.

Herbs, like basil, thyme, oregano, sage and dill, all love the heat and will perform better as spring progresses. Mints, which can be quite aggressive in ground, are more well behaved in containers. Containing mint and using it is a great way to enjoy a mojito or a cold glass of mint iced tea after work.

Sometimes, you do everything right, and you still don't have success with a certain plant. Perhaps the weather gets too hot too soon, or the sun never seems to shine long enough to have a ripened tomato. In my state, spring weather can last a long time, or it can end before May. In spring, I rarely get a crop of beets for example, but I love the color of 'Bull's Blood' beet foliage. I use it with my ornamental plants and just before it begins to bolt – flower – I cut the leaves and eat them as nutritious salad greens. By learning to eat other parts of a vegetable plant, you aren't losing any of your time, effort or taste.

Fall

Fall is the time for reaping the rewards of your small kitchen garden. Before the first frost, gather in vegetables that still remain. They've still got more to give you.

⇨ **TOMATOES.** Harvest green tomatoes and eat them in relishes, salsas or even fried. Or, cut them from the mother plant, leaving some stem and cap on the tomato. Separate those that are whitish – which means they have started the ripening process – from the really hard, green ones. Wrap these in paper – newspaper is great – and put them in a paper bag. Store them somewhere dark and cool like a basement or closet. The cooler the temperature, the slower they will ripen. If you want to speed up the process, place an apple in a sack with them. Check on tomatoes weekly to see if any are beginning to spoil, and discard those.

⇨ PEPPERS. Freeze peppers by cutting them in half, removing stems and seeds. Place them in bags, labeled with variety and date and store in the freezer. You can enjoy peppers all winter this way, and it's cheaper than buying peppers at the store.

TIP: If you planted your hot and mild peppers near each other, they will probably all be hot in the second generation.

⇨ OKRA. A great way to save okra is to slice it and then freeze on a cookie sheet for twenty-four hours. Slide frozen okra pieces into a baggie. They will stay separate and can be used in soups and stews or breaded and fried.

Saving seed is a fall joy. Dry a couple of those peppers if you want to save seeds, unless they are hybrids, of course. The same holds true for beans and peas, but tomato seed saving is a different process. (See how to on page 78). I usually wait to gather pepper seeds from plants until right after the first freeze when peppers are dried on the plant.

I store seeds in paper envelopes or small bags. Be sure any seeds you save are labeled properly because, you won't remember their names in February. Store seeds in the refrigerator or another cool place.

It's clean-up time. Fall is also the time to clean up and move on. Gardening is a seasonal process. No matter what happened this season, if you've learned one or two new skills, it was a good year. I know it's hard to say goodbye to the garden, but try to enjoy all it has to offer in each season. When you go outside, focus all of your senses on the world around you. Listen to birds singing. Feel breezes, now beginning to cool, on your neck. Rub fuzzy leaves beneath your fingertips. Breathe in the scents of ripened vegetables, herbs and fruit. Notice how the green leaves turn into the brilliant, rich hues of fall.

Winterize your garden. Before winter sets in, clean out dead leaves and other debris from your containers. While plastic pots will be fine on the deck throughout winter – at least for a couple of seasons – terra cotta can chip and break in winter freeze/thaw cycles. I bring all of my glazed containers up next to the house in late fall, off of my elevated deck. I also turn over any empty pots and keep them in a covered area. If you want to remove potting soil and stack the containers out of sight, that's fine too. Dump used potting soil into a covered trash can or other receptacle so you can mix it with new potting soil in the spring. Be sure to clean and put away all tools, too. I place mine in clear plastic stacking boxes. These are very handy because they allow me to see my tools from all sides.

Winterize your hoses. Break down whatever watering system you've used. If you don't unhook your outdoor hoses and drain them, they may burst and be unusable next year. The same holds true for hose end sprayers and sprinklers. Store them inside where they won't freeze. One year, I forgot to unhook my hoses, and the faucet on my house froze and burst back into the wall. That was an expensive repair and a hard lesson. If you installed a drip system this year, break it down and store emitters and hoses with other water supplies. If you have a lot of pots, make a quick map of how you laid out your system. It will save a great deal of time next year. I like to tape my map to the box holding the drip system. In warmer parts of the country, you may not need to break down the system; just drain it and leave in place.

Overwintering potted shrubs and trees

If you're overwintering shrubs and trees in pots, you will want to bring them close to the house. You can put some plants in the garage if you have one, but honestly, I find that the east side of the house works even better (unless you live in a brutal winter climate). This also takes advantage of winter sunlight. Water these overwintered plants once a month. Roots still grow when soil temperatures are 41°F or higher.

For any tropical tree or shrub you want to save, bring it indoors and place in a sunny window. I have windows on the east and west sides of my house, and the sunlight from the west windows really heats up in winter. Be sure to turn any plants you have indoors every other week to take advantage of the light. Don't be too alarmed if plants drop leaves. As long as you continue to water and turn them, chances are good that you can save that Meyer lemon tree for next year. It will be set back for the beginning of the season, though.

* * *

Way to go!

If you live in a warm climate, you may want to continue gardening throughout winter. We'll talk more about extending the harvest in the next chapter.

Chapter Three

The Year of Achieving Container Wisdom and Expanding Your Horizons

Now's the year to just go for it. We'll talk about outsmarting your climate, the bad bugs and the good bugs, freedom through drip irrigation, hybrid seeds vs. heirlooms... and the joys of going beyond veggies and growing your own fruits and fruit trees in pots.

HOW WAS YOUR SECOND YEAR OF GARDEN GOODNESS? Depending upon the weather in your area, you may feel quite happy, or "chuffed," as my British friends say. If not, no worries. Hang in there. Every year you learn more. I've been gardening for thirty-plus years, and I'm still learning.

Gardens are metaphors for life. There are good times and bad. The weather may be golden one month and disastrous the next. Corn earworms may ravage your crop or squash bugs decimate your zucchini, but we gardeners soldier on. Those golden moments of harvest are what we savor. It is the joy we feel when we taste the peas and potatoes we grew. Nothing tastes like food you just harvested yourself. Some seeds, like 'Dragon Tongue' beans and 'Nevada lettuce' become old and steady friends even as we stretch our wings and greet new seed varieties each season. Gardening holds simple joys, and if everyone knew what we had, they would race to grab a tool and help.

Unfortunately, they don't know. Just like parenting or any other life endeavor, you don't know how worthy it is until you do it, and no one can explain it to you until they do it themselves.

Don't let unseasonable weather get you down

You know how *A Tale of Two Cities* starts with the line, "It was the best of times, it was worst of times?" I maintain he was talking about my garden around seed-starting time. My climate has the best of weather and the worst of weather. It is the best because I'm in the USDA Zone 7A/6B belt that runs across our county, meaning I can grow nearly everything, from artichokes to lettuce, from pumpkins to corn, and most fruits. But I also live on the prairie, which means our weather is extremely variable. With a cold front, the temperature can change 50 degrees in a matter of minutes. We have years with good rainfall, but we also have 3 to 5 year droughts every 5 or 10 years.

I must prepare my garden for nearly every weather variation, and sometimes I feel like a superhero when I manage to eke anything out of the soil. That's the truth. Other years, I can't help but grow amazing food and flowers, so much that I must either freeze, can or give to the local food bank what my family can't use. Two summers ago, I had so many peaches I peeled and froze six bags in one afternoon. The next May, a record-setting late freeze killed off any dreams of peaches. Last year, we had so many organic apples on our single 'Enterprise' tree that I begged friends to come pick. This summer, I counted four apples on four trees.

Gardening is sometimes frustrating, but the work is of great value. The disappointing years shouldn't prevent you from enjoying the bountiful ones. The best teacher for a crazy climate is simply time. To help your garden now, learn to plant seeds from last frost charts and check with local weather and agricultural boards to see what weather-tracking systems are available in your area. Oklahoma uses Mesonet, a network of environmental monitoring systems that allows you to track weather trends and ground temperatures; other states may have something similar. This knowledge can help you plan the best times to plant.

Bad bugs, Good Bugs and Some That Are In-Between

We've talked about weather. Now, let's discuss the creepy crawlies of the ecosystem you've created outdoors. First, give yourself a pat on the back. If you plant vegetables, herbs and simple flowers, you are aiding our ecosystem. Pollinators that once depended upon nectar and other food in fields throughout America have fewer choices every year. By planting a garden of any kind – grown without chemicals – you are helping them reproduce, and that's a good thing.

I was once afraid of insects, flying ones in particular. Good gardens, especially those in the South, really buzz in spring and summer, and it took all of my courage to go out there and work. I am a foodie, though, and I love flowers. This gave me the determination to deadhead and tie up plants while dragonflies and other winged insects flitted about my head and hands. Over time, I've become more interested in the pollinators than I ever thought I would. Sometimes, seeing certain insects fluttering about the garden makes me stop what I'm doing and just watch.

I have great sympathy for beginning gardeners who reach for a can of bug spray upon seeing an insect devouring their precious plants. Mistrust of bugs seems to be part of our DNA. But you have to set aside this fear and see the bugs for what they are: part of your garden's ecosystem. They are even vital to its survival. Did you know even stinging insects won't hurt you while they're at work sipping nectar

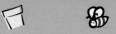

in the garden? They are far too busy to bother with stinging you. If you're still concerned, study insect behavior and learn which insects are more likely to sting and why. I did.

The main problem with bugs arises when bad bugs outnumber good ones, and your garden suffers. Really irritating insect pests, like potato bugs, grasshoppers, asparagus beetles, squash bugs, and coddling moths, all damage plants. You work so hard to get your veggies to fruit, and a grasshopper eats them down to the nubs. I am familiar with this upsetting reality. In my garden, 2013 was the "Year of the Grasshopper." Sheesh!

Before you reach for a spray, organic or not, take a moment to know your enemy. Some insects look really fierce and frightening, but they're only a problem for the insects they eat. Others look cute and cuddly – some baby moths, for example – but they will cut down your gardening efforts in a day. You might even decide that for special creatures, like checkerspot or swallowtail butterfly caterpillars, you're willing to give them a plant or two in order for you to enjoy the adults later. If you love swallowtails, I'll just tell you now: plant extra dill, fennel and parsley. Their caterpillars love dill – to death.

Here are some common garden insects that can be good, bad or somewhere in-between. Actually, I don't like the good-bad marker. The health of a garden all depends upon balance.

Beneficial Insects

The best way to invite these helpers into your garden is to throw them a party. Discover what adults like to eat and drink, and before long, you'll have plenty of beneficial insects taking care of business in your vegetable plot. Here are three I see much of the growing season:

⇨ **LADYBUGS OR LADY BEETLES.** We all love adult lady beetles, partly because we were introduced to them in childhood by such books as *The Grouchy Ladybug,* by Eric Carle. But many of us have squished a baby lady beetle accidentally, thinking it was something killing our plants instead of killing aphids. Immature ladybugs are called lions, and they do look fierce; however, they eat more aphids than the adults – 50 or more per day. In the spring, when aphids are at their worst, we may be tempted to get out the bug spray. However, in a balanced ecosystem, lady beetles and lacewings (another beneficial) will get rid of those aphids in no time, and without harmful sprays. If you decide to buy either for your garden from your local nursery or online, they come in a small box and are ravenous. Spray your plants with sugar water right before releasing them in the evening. This entices these helpful bugs to stay, mate and make more little lions.

⇨ **LACEWINGS.** The adults don't eat much except for pollen and nectar. However, their larvae (also called lions) are voracious. I have bought ladybugs, but not lacewings. Lacewings simply show up, and I do my best not to interfere with their work; if you do want to buy them, they comein several different life stages including larvae in a small bottle. Weird, huh?

⇨ **PARASITIC WASPS.** There isn't just one species; there are many. Female wasps lay eggs in caterpillars or other host insects, and the wasp larvae devour the host from the inside out. I've actually seen a tomato hornworm covered in wasp larvae. It was gross, but fascinating. I didn't see this unusual sight (or the adult wasps) until I gardened organically for a few years, but it was awesome when I did.

⇨ **THE POLLINATORS.** There are thousands more beneficial insects than the three I mentioned – the pollinators, especially. Pollinators, that large group of insects that buzz from one plant to another, are as important to your garden as those who are bug-eat-bug. They go about their busy lives sipping nectar and pollinating your crops. So, the next time a bee or wasp buzzes by you in the garden, try not to jump. Instead, say thank you. I know you're already being nice to the butterflies, moths and hummingbirds. They're much more cuddly.

Pain in the a _ _ (PITA) insects

⇨ **SPIDER MITES.** These tiny, horrible little creatures want to suck the life out of your garden when summer weather turns hot and dry. Regular insecticides don't work, so don't even try them. Spider mites are a real problem on my hollies and rose bushes, so I go out every morning when it's hot and spray them with blasts of water. Neem oil also helps by smothering them, but in a hot climate it burns plant leaves. Plus, it's a generalized control and kills beneficials, too.

⇨ **CUTWORMS.** My word, I hate these irritating creatures. They are a real problem at the beginning of gardening season. You don't often see them because they do most of their damage at night. You will know they've been there, however, when you find a small plant chewed in half nearly at ground level. This happens most often right after you've set out a small transplant. But don't despair – I have good news: these larvae are easy to dissuade. You simply place something hard right next to the plant's stem after you've put it in the hole. You can use a nail, but honestly, I'm usually in a hurry at transplanting time and don't have a nail handy. So, I started placing plant

tags right next to the stem, and – voila! It worked. Later, when the plant has grown, remove the tag and place it where you can identify your plant more easily. Believe it or not, one tag or nail will do the job because the caterpillar/cutworm can't encircle the plant's stem and cut it in half.

⇨ **GRASSHOPPERS.** In hot, dry climates, grasshoppers can quickly become a menace. I use Nolo bait during bad years. It is a pathogen that causes insects – including grasshoppers, locusts and crickets – to slow their feeding and eventually die. The disease is carried on wheat bran, and grasshoppers belly up to the buffet when the bait is spread (see the Resources section for where to purchase Nolo bait.) Grasshoppers aren't a problem in some places, but in Oklahoma they can resemble the plagues of Egypt. Use your discretion when deciding how to deal with these potential pests.

Generalized predator bugs: neither good nor bad

Every garden has its share of predator insects deemed either good or bad, depending upon what they're eating. Here are two:

⇨ **ASSASSIN BUG OR WHEEL BUG.** So named because of the wheel on its back, assassin bugs are tremendous predators. These large, intimidating bugs will eat any bug that crosses their paths. They also fly. Even though they do eat destructive insects, I am not very fond of them. Here's why. When disturbed, they drop to the ground, and if you accidentally squish one while you're pulling weeds, it will bite you and perhaps not even die. I also find them eating lots of pollinators, who are busy doing their work and not paying attention. Assassin bugs, although classified as "good bugs," eat more pollinators in my garden than destructive pests. This will be controversial with some gardeners, but some years, when these aggressive bugs take over the garden, I have been known to take my clippers and cut a few in half to decrease their numbers and even the score. I do not feel guilty about this.

⇨ **PRAYING MANTIS.** We tend to love this insect because of its oddly shaped head and ability to watch us as we work. However, like assassin bugs, they are generalized predators. If you have a lot of praying mantises in your garden, you may soon see them with butterflies in their mouths. I don't ever have too many praying mantises, so I don't classify them as either good or bad. Use your own judgment if you feel mantises are too much of a problem in your garden.

Managing Garden Pests Organically

There are two primary options for dealing with garden pests organically: integrated pest management and biological pest controls. If you're an organic gardener, or want to be one, you should understand these two schools of thought and how to use them when dealing with insect pests:

Integrated Pest Management. IPM is a technical term meaning "Do the least harm first." People who practice IPM analyze the situation before they apply anything to the garden. Just because a gardener sees one insect doesn't mean it's an invasion. Part of this method is tolerance and deciding how much damage you can stand before you step in. Obviously, cutworms do their work quickly, but you can replant and use the barrier strategy I mentioned earlier. No need for spray. You are practicing IPM when you rotate crops, plant disease-resistant cultivars that perform well in your area, and welcome beneficial insects. Keeping your plants healthy by mulching, using compost and watering is also an IPM practice, since healthy plants are more resistant to disease and insects. One of the best things you can do for your garden is to visit it every day. You begin to know your plants and can quickly spot a problem.

Biological Pest Controls. This is a formal term for a simple practice. When you use beneficial insects as predators, along with parasites and diseases specific to a particular insect, you are using biological pest controls. In doing so, you don't harm other insects, birds or fish. But I don't use even biological controls until I've exhausted hand-picking – with gloves. If that doesn't work, I use biological controls like *Bacillus thuringiensis,* known as Bt (naturally-occurring bacteria that make caterpillars sick), for really pesky caterpillar/tobacco hornworm invasions, and Nolo bait for grasshoppers. Before using any of these, follow all directions carefully so the control has the best effect and doesn't hurt other insects or animals.

There are organic pesticides, but even these have consequences. I don't spray anything unless I simply must.

Over the years, things have become pretty balanced through good garden practices, along with the encouragement of beneficial insects. Plus, I have twenty chickens who would just love to eat a bug or two. Hand-picked insects are a delicacy to them.

If you've used chemicals in the past, don't feel bad. The lure of the "dark force" is strong. However, the next time you're compelled to get out a spray, even if it is organic, jump on the Internet and educate yourself first by reading good information from agricultural universities or local cooperative extension services. Try some of the links in the Resources section, too. Get to know your garden. For, as author Maya Angelou says, "When you know better you do better."

Dealing with disease

When gardening in containers, I don't find my plants suffer much disease. If a season is too rainy, perhaps, but otherwise there isn't much trouble. The lowest leaves on tomato plants sometimes die from disease, and if this occurs, I remove and dispose of them. *Caution:* don't put diseased plant material in the compost pile, as they can affect the whole batch. There are organic sprays you can use to combat disease, but good air circulation and keeping leaves dry go a long way in prevention. Also, make sure plants have enough nutrients and water. These simple practices will lead to healthy, happy plants and a good harvest.

Two Smart Ways to Get Water to Your Plants

Drip Irrigation

Do you like to travel? Vacations worry gardeners, but with drip irrigation, it is easy to keep pots happy. Drip irrigation is also efficient and environmentally sound.

My nephew once house-sat and watered our garden, but he got married a couple of years ago and is no longer available to care for the plants while I'm away. To make sure the pots were still watered, Bill and I installed a drip system last summer. It took about an hour to complete this task, it wasn't hard at all, and it was worth it for our peace of mind.

What you'll need:

⇨ **DRIP IRRIGATION KIT** with a backflow preventer, tubing, fittings and drip emitters.

⇨ **BRASS Y-ATTACHMENT.**

⇨ **BATTERY-OPERATED TIMER** to set for daily watering.

⇨ **FILTER** to trap particles and stop clogged emitters.

⇨ **PRESSURE REGULATOR** so the system won't blow out from too much pressure. And possibly a pressure fitting to connect the tubing to the regulator.

⇨ **DRIP EMITTERS** in varying rates. I use larger emitters of up to two gallons per hour for larger pots.

What to do:

Set up your system to water at night or early morning when plants are less stressed. Use ½-inch black polyethylene tubing as the main line and hide it if you want. Mine isn't very well hidden, but no one notices it among the jungle of green plants and pots.

Run microtubing to each pot. Once these are set in place, secure with a pin or hose spikes; pierce the main tubing.

Test your system by running it for ten minutes or longer until you get the desired rate. Soil should be thoroughly soaked, with water draining out of the container.

You can set the timer so pots will be watered twice a day, if necessary.

Self-watering containers

If you don't want to invest in drip irrigation, you might try self-watering containers, like EarthBox® or Grow-Box™ systems. With these, you fill up a reservoir of water that can last up to a week without further watering. See the Resources for details. They may not be exactly beautiful, but they have a lot going for them.

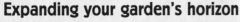

Expanding your garden's horizon

Once you start harvesting good food, you'll want to change things up so you can grow a greater variety. Competition with the neighbors' garden can be a good motivator, too. It's always fun to try growing different vegetables, fruit and flowers than your friendly competitor over the fence (or the adjacent deck).

But before you invest time and labor into that pack of seeds, you should know something about the varieties that are available to you, and something about their background. It's a big help if you are familiar with some common garden terminology. Read on.

Hybrids vs. Heirlooms: the great debate

There's an ongoing debate in this country regarding heirlooms and hybrids, and no, I'm not talking cars.

Hybrids

Before the term GMO entered our modern vernacular and caused so much hoopla, conversation stewed over hybrid plants and seeds vs. heirlooms and open-pollinated varieties. Hybrids were touted as the wave of the future when they were first developed. They were going to solve world hunger and make the planet a safer and better place. Sound familiar?

While I don't think hybrids should be credited with superhero qualities, they do live up to some of their hype. Often, a hybrid will contain genetic qualities that infuse it with better disease resistance and increased vigor.

Why were hybrids developed? Partly because of shipping. People wanted food transported across the country, and growers and hybridizers wanted them to have it. The tomato, for example. Tomatoes, at one time, were too thin-skinned and fragile to be crated and shipped long distances and still arrive looking fresh and beautiful. Enter the 'Big Boy' tomato. This hybrid has been in constant production since 1949. It was bred for consistency in fruit size and shape, redness and productivity. And toughness.

Is a hybrid a GMO, then? No. Hybrids are not genetically modified organisms (GMOs.) Hybrids are controlled crosses of two parent plant varieties. F1 hybrids are even more controlled crosses from inbred lines and can be patented by hybridizers. To keep the same F1 plant, the same cross must be made each year. Hybrids are heavily marketed to farmers, but home gardeners may find they like a particular F1 hybrid, too. Don't try to save seed from a hybrid because it won't breed true to its mother plant. Save seeds from varieties that are open-pollinated (see Glossary).

GMOs, on the other hand, involve gene splicing from different species and change a plant's DNA, often to withstand chemical sprays and other applications. Are you confused yet? Basically, hybrids use the entire genetic information of two parent plants, and GMOs don't. I do plant some hybrids, but I DO NOT grow GMO plants.

Why grow hybrids? In my climate with its long summers, you would think tomatoes are easy and prolific. Not so, grasshopper. From year to year, tomato production is iffy because we are often plagued with temperatures over 100°F in early summer. Go above that number, and tomato blossoms drop to the ground to die a lonely and unfulfilled death. Some hybrids, like 'Early Girl' and 'Celebrity' mature early, while others, like 'Defiant', are resistant to late blight, the same disease that caused the Irish potato famine. Late blight was a huge problem for gardeners in the Eastern U.S. in 2009 and 2012 and has the potential to spread throughout the U.S. While none of the above hybrids are personal favorites, I plant 'Supersteak' and 'Jet Star' each spring. Each is tasty, dependable and prolific, three qualities I like best in a vegetable plant. If you take up space in my garden, you'd better perform.

Decoding hybrid information. Hybrid tomatoes often sport initials like: V, F, N, T and A, meaning they have resistance to verticillium wilt, fusarium wilt, nematode disease, tobacco mosaic virus and alternaria. (Become a gardener, and not only will you be an amateur botanist, but a biologist and chemist, too.) And there are other tomato viruses, including leaf problems; so now there are more letters on some seed packets. It's good to know what they mean.

BCTV – beet curly top virus resistance

SWV – tomato spotted wilt virus resistance

LB – late blight resistance

Heirlooms may not have those fancy letters behind their colorful names, but they, too, can develop resistance to some diseases, depending upon where they're grown.

Heirlooms

Now, you heirloom enthusiasts, I see you standing there with your pitchforks, tar and feathers . . . just hold off a minute. Count me in as a feverish fanatic, too. Who can resist the romantic history and sheer oddity of heirlooms? I'm the first to say that if you want to grow something really different, try an heirloom.

What is an heirloom plant? Well, the definition changes depending upon who you talk to. There is the dictionary definition – plant varieties fifty years and older – but it sounds like the dusty definition for antique furniture. Heirlooms actually change every year you grow them, especially if you save seed. Some are passed down through the generations of a family and are really good for a particular area of the country. Others are old varieties that were used in farmers markets long ago. Still others are seeds found by plantsmen and women who travel to far-off places to track them down.

Heirlooms are open-pollinated, but not all open-pollinated seeds are straight out of history. When buying open-pollinated seeds, consider choosing a company that tests its seeds in a climate similar to yours. Although I buy seeds from many different places, I tend to buy heirlooms and other open-pollinated seeds from Southern companies that test their seeds in a climate like mine. Heirloom tomatoes I particularly like are 'Black Krim,' a dark Russian beefsteak, and 'Cherokee Purple,' another "black" tomato that grows large, rich fruit.

Grafted tomatoes burst on the scene recently, and I'm hearing good things about them. However, that's another debate for another time. Choose your veggie seed wisely. Ask questions of farmers at your local market. They often pass on knowledge to new gardeners about specific varieties that perform well. Join a vegetable garden club and talk to members. You'll find they love to share their knowledge and seeds.

Also, if you have a seed company still near you, count your lucky stars, for you are fortunate indeed. We had one for years, Horn Seed, and along the back wall where drawers of bulk seed sat, was the best place to talk tomatoes, okra, corn and other good things. When Horn Seed burned a couple of years ago, a groan was heard throughout my state. There will never be anything like it locally again.

Chat up your neighbor across the fence, especially if he or she has a vegetable garden. Although neighbors may not lead you in all the right places, I've found gardeners are among the most generous people in the world. They not only share – unload – their zucchini in the summer, they'll tell you what seed produces the most flavorful veggies. In a few short years, you'll be sharing your knowledge with others, too, and arguing over the best hot or sweet peppers.

Believe me, you will.

Growing Small Fruits

Did you know many fruits are easy to grow in containers? Some, like blueberries, have special soil requirements, but growing small fruits may be easier than you think. And if you have alkaline soil like I do, pots may be the only way to grow.

Here's what I would grow in pots:

Blueberries

You'll need more than one variety to get a good fruit set. You can get a bit of fruit from one plant, but more is better. Blueberries also have beautiful foliage that turns a lovely bronze in fall.

Sun: Blueberries can do well in a hot climate if they get morning light and shelter from afternoon sun. In less harsh climates, make sure plants have full sun, meaning 6 to 8 hours.

How many? Plant at least three shrubs of different cultivars near each other. I planted two different cultivars in a large pot on my deck and have another cultivar nearby for additional pollination.

Planting instructions: Use ½ regular potting soil and ½ acid soil, or add sulphur to the soil based upon the size of pot. Blueberries aren't heavy feeders. Just give them some organic granulated fertilizer when you plant and each spring thereafter. If leaves start to yellow during growing season, you may need to test your soil and add sulphur to your container. Around my smallish blueberry plants, I plant blooming flowers like trailing petunias for visual impact. They won't compete with the blueberries, and they round out the container garden nicely.

Care: In my Zone 7 garden, I don't bring plants indoors. I hug them up against the house, where they sit all cozy until spring comes again. My blueberry plants are tough. They even grow well in wintery climates like Maine, but remember that growing in containers is much colder in the winter for plants than growing them in soil. The temperature drop is equivalent to about two zones colder. You may want to wrap the pots in bubble wrap if you leave them outdoors (For zone info, see www.planthardiness.ars.usda.gov/).

Which cultivar? Blueberries do need some winter chill to produce berries. Some cultivars need more than others. I grow 'Top Hat,' which is 2 feet by 3 feet and grows in Zones 4 to 7. "Peach Sorbet™" has beautiful foliage color and works very well in pots. 'Sunshine Blue' was bred for more southern climates (Zones 4 to 9). "Jelly Bean™" is another dwarf variety you can consider.

Raspberries

Unlike blueberries, raspberries want neutral soil. They are also deciduous, which means their leaves drop in late fall, so don't worry that your plant is dying when its foliage vanishes.

Sun: My raspberries grow on my deck next to the dwarf blueberries. Oklahoma summers are harsh, so I make sure they get morning sun. In more temperate climates, grow them in full sun, 6 to 8 hours per day.

How many? Raspberries are self-pollinating. You only need one, but you might plant two just because you want more berries.

Planting Instructions: Regular potting soil is just fine for raspberries. However, don't get confused and use garden soil instead. It doesn't have the right drainage requirements and should only be used in gardens. Place each raspberry shrub in a large container, between 24-36 inches and even larger, because even smaller cultivars will grow quite large. Place the plant in the container so that the soil level is even with the top of the root ball.

Care: These plants enjoy full sun, except during hotter summers, when you should move them to where they'll receive only morning sun. They need soil that is well drained. Fertilize early in the spring with a balanced liquid fertilizer and water moderately throughout the season.

Which cultivar? I like Raspberry Shortcake™, a dwarf cultivar that grows 2 to 3 feet tall and prefers Zones 5 to 9 for containers. It's great for children because the canes are thornless. If you want to grow a more traditional raspberry, you'll need a trellis for the canes. You can try black and golden raspberry varieties, too.

Dwarf Fruit Trees

Since we're talking about fruit, why not plant a small fruit tree? Do you like apples, or have you wanted to try figs? What about Meyer lemons, or limes for margaritas or guacamole? Do you dream of peach cobbler with ice cream? Then peaches might be your favorite summer fruit? Here's the good news: you can plant any of the above in a container and be very successful. Whichever you choose, remember that containers need protection during winter. For tropical fruits, that means moving pots indoors or to a greenhouse. For other fruits, it means lining them up on the east side of the house or building where they are sheltered from cold winter winds.

Apple

With apple trees, the main thing to remember is that they are not self-pollinating like a peach or a plum. So, you will either need two trees that will pollinate each other, or a tree with different varieties grafted onto the main trunk. When you call a nursery to order, ask for a dwarf or columnar tree, along with varieties that cross-pollinate.

Peach

As for peach trees, choose the cultivar you want to grow by searching farmers' markets for those varieties you most like to eat. Peach varieties in the grocery section are picked specifically for their ability to ship long distances, a fact that holds true for most fruit and vegetables in the stores. That's why some of them taste like cardboard. If you're going to grow your own, get one you'd love to take a bite out of, rather than one that will travel well. I have two different peach trees I grow in my front lawn, and in the years when we don't get a late freeze, they make a delicious harvest. However, knowing what I do now, I would plant a freestone variety grafted to dwarf rootstock. My peaches are clingy, and they are difficult to peel and put up in the freezer.

I would try a cultivar like 'Southern Sweet,' a freestone dwarf variety that produces medium-sized fruits. There are so many varieties of peaches. Some are self-fertile. Others need a companion tree to produce good fruit. Still, a summer without peaches isn't really summer to me.

In early spring, you can plant either bare-root trees or trees that come in nursery pots. Either way, choose a good nursery that knows what you want, and tell them you are going to grow these trees in containers. Use a large container so your tree has plenty of room. Don't go any smaller than 20 inches in diameter for a dwarf fruit tree. Roots don't mind being bound, but you don't want to have to replant often, either.

If the plant is bare-root, take it out of the container and soak the roots for an hour first. If it's a potted plant in a container, knock the sides of the nursery pot to loosen it and carefully pull the tree out.

For a bare-root tree or other bare-root plants (such as roses), make a cone in the potting soil and arrange the roots around it. Place more soil around the roots so that the tree is standing straight in the pot. For a container plant, shake some of the soil from the roots and place the tree in the container. Cover roots with soil up to where the tree trunk meets its roots.

Water the tree and watch for the soil to settle. If you have any spots that indicate air pockets, place more soil and again water.

Even though it may seem challenging, try growing a fruit tree. Think of how impressed your friends and family will be when you bake an apple pie with fruit from your own garden or pluck a 'Meyer' lemon for their iced tea. Deliver a basket of peaches from your back yard and watch their reaction. Growing your own fruit is sweet, indeed.

* * *

Way to go!

In your first year, you learned to listen to Spring's siren song, but how to avoid the pitfalls of the beginner. You now know your site, how to choose containers, which potting soil to use, and how to water. You can decipher a seed packet, and you know which vegetables to purchase as transplants and those that can be sown as seeds. Maybe you even tried Project Salad Bowl. I hope so.

Next, you focused upon your second growing season – unless you read and worked ahead. If so, that's just fine! I want you to move back and forth through the book in whatever fashion works for you. Gardening isn't a linear thing, and many skills overlap. We started seeds indoors and discussed growing what you really want or need to eat, including exploring cuisines from around the world. We went through the seasons in your garden and learned how to make compost or manure tea.

I hope that by the end of your third year in Garden 1, you have expanded your horizons and will try some of the techniques you learned in all three chapters, along with some fruit shrubs and trees or unique vegetables. Variety is part of the equation and makes gardening fun.

You may find at the end of this section that you've fallen in love with growing plants in containers, and you can't imagine gardening any other way even if you move to a house with a yard or a larger space. Many gardeners, especially those living in large urban areas with tall buildings, grow whole landscapes with pots and on rooftops. It's a great way to grow food and flowers in what can be a cold setting of concrete, asphalt and steel. Even so, I hope you'll enjoy Garden 2, which has ideas that can also be applied to container gardening since raised beds, which are the mainstay of Garden 2, are just bigger containers. It's not that much of a stretch, but you'll be able to grow more food.

You may also long for a bit of land to call your own. I know I did when I lived in an apartment. Garden 2 addresses your longing for more and shows you how to do it once you get your first home. But you don't need that home in order to read and dream about it. I bought my first gardening books when I was still living in a dorm in college because they gave me respite from studying and helped me fashion the garden I later called home.

> **"A modest garden contains, for those who know how to look and to wait,**
> **more instruction than a library."**
>
> – Henri Frederic Amiel

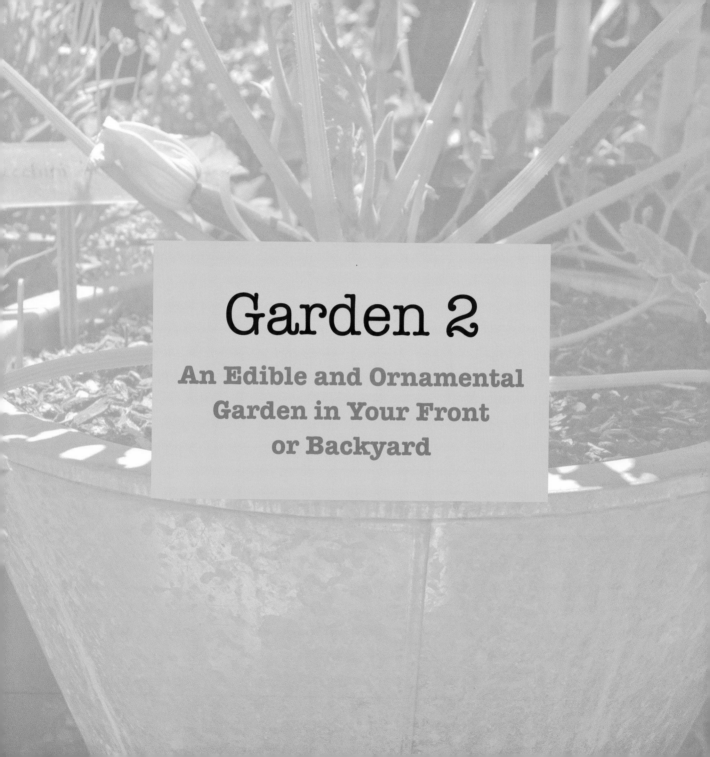

Chapter Four

Looking at Design

Who says you can't have it all - veggies, flowers and drop-dead gorgeousness?
Now that you've got a little more room to spread your gardening wings, we'll
look at front and backyard design, integrating flowers into the veggie patch,
what to plant where, creating raised beds, starting an herb garden.... and
I'll give you my Top 10 List of Beautiful Edibles.

THE DESIGN IDEAS YOU'RE ABOUT TO SEE ARE ALL ABOUT MIXING PRACTICALITY WITH BEAUTY. (That's my own veggie garden on the previous page, which evolved over a period of time and more than one complete redesign.) You've seen purely ornamental gardens, with their lavish flowers and lush foliage. You've probably also encountered the traditional vegetable patch, where every plant has a use and earns its plot of soil by the bounty it produces. The goal of Garden 2 is to help you marry these two concepts and create a garden that is pretty, practical and, most importantly, doable. Adapt these ideas to suit your space and needs. Anything counts, from a one-container herb garden to a collection of raised beds. This is about designing a garden that works for you and your home.

I've called plenty of places home. Once I waved good-bye to my parents, I lived in a dorm room for a year, a mobile home for five, an apartment for a short time, and later, my own house. I've only lived in two houses, one

in the suburbs and the other out in the countryside, where I live now. In every space, I made sure to plant something to make it feel like home. When I bought my first house I was so excited. I signed on the dotted line and then ran around my postage-stamp front and backyard practically doing handsprings. Finally, I had the space to grow and grow some more!

No matter what space you call home, you can still make it yours. A few packets of seeds and a bit of determination can make for a beautiful garden of any size you desire. This chapter will get you started designing an edible and ornamental garden, and the next two will show you how to build upon your success for seasons to come. Soon, you'll have a beautiful harvest. Nothing says "home" better than a harvest of flowers and food.

What to Plant Where

A sunny space is paramount to vegetable growing. Vegetables, as we discussed before, are annuals and they love the sun. Many actually hail from the tropics, so you know they're programmed for sunshine. Ideally, every potential vegetable gardener would have a sunny yard to satisfy these plants' needs. Sometimes, though, trees shade a yard, making vegetable growing a bit trickier. But shade can be good, too; some plants like leafy greens prefer to be out of direct sunlight especially as the weather warms. Grow these in your garden, and you can embrace your shade-producing trees.

You may find that the best spot for planting vegetables is your front yard. Wherever you decide to grow, try to place your garden close to the house so you can see it from a window. You'll be much more likely to dash out and pull an errant weed or two if you can see your plot from inside your home.

Bumping up against restrictions. Before you build raised beds in your front yard or till it up with a rented tiller, check your homeowner's association regulations and local city ordinances. I know it sounds crazy, but many people are terribly attached to their carpets of green lawn, and you may be prohibited from growing vegetables instead. You don't want to invest hard work in this project only to have some city official with a weed-eater knocking down your corn or tomatoes. You may also be fined. If you encounter resistance, try presenting your reasons for a front yard garden at your homeowners' or town council meeting; you could be the catalyst for change. If your request is denied, look for another place to garden, but keep trying to win over neighbors and

city officials to the revolutionary idea that vegetable gardens can be beautiful *and* functional. That's how a group of motivated citizens in Oklahoma City managed to get urban chickens back in residential yards. They worked for several years, but finally convinced the city to allow chickens, though with certain restrictions. Sadly, the ordinance was later rescinded. A brief victory for those of us who want to live a life more connected to domesticated poultry and the soil.

Creative sneakiness. If you find you have to work within regulations, try this creative approach: sneak your veggies into your ornamental landscape. Some vegetables and fruits are so attractive they form their own camouflage. Hiding your green peppers beneath some ornamental foliage allows you to abide by city restrictions and homeowner covenants while still being able to enjoy a productive garden. I'm not rabidly anti-lawn, but I find lawn carpets boring. Too much restful space for the eyes. I want to be surrounded by interesting plants and structures – and vegetable gardens provide that. Tuck vegetables into ornamental landscapes here and there like my friend, Shawna Coronado, did here.

Maybe your lawn could slowly disappear inch-by-inch, and an ornamental and productive garden gradually take its place. You have options, and you're smart. Your generation will change how we look at property and at the never-ending lawn that presently covers our country. Productive gardens are the future, and you can lead the way.

Peaceful coexistence. Most residential neighborhoods have a certain feel. Working within that framework instead of against it can take extra planning, but it's worth it. Suburbia is empty and spacious and just waiting for a little spicing up. Backyards often have green planted borders along the edge of the fenced property with a green space in the middle. Those borders are usually filled with ornamental shrubs and small trees, both of which have root systems that may be large enough to inhibit planting a vegetable garden around them.

If your home is new construction, or if some of these border plants are overgrown or diseased and need to be replaced, here's my suggestion: install blooming shrubs and small trees in their place instead of the ordinary wallpaper of green. Why shrubs and trees that bloom? They encourage pollinators, which are essential to a productive vegetable garden. And it's not just fruit trees that have blossoms; other trees do, too.

Save your veggies for where you have plenty of space. Purely ornamental plants aren't all bad. They provide structure in the landscape for example. Flowering bushes and trees announce spring to the neighborhood and cheer us at the end of winter. Everyone should have at least one blooming tree in their yard, and maybe more. Shrubs like our native American beautybush, have berries birds love, and perennials provide cover for nesting sites. Birds, in turn, help rid your garden of excess bugs, which is another great thing. Productive gardens are valuable, but don't forget that ornamental plants help keep your garden beautiful, healthy *and* in line with the requirements of traditional suburban neighborhoods.

How can you tell if your plants are too hot, overwatered or underwatered?

Wilted plants with drooping, sad leaves are the first signal that your plants either need water or more shade. Spring plants like lettuce and spinach will also try to flower (bolt). However, plants can also droop if they're overwatered, so how can you tell the difference? Use your senses of touch, sight and smell. Push your index finger into the soil to feel if it is wet or dry. Sniff the area for a foul smell of rotting vegetation. Note whether your plant is standing in water, or if the area around it is dry.

Rule of thumb:

⇨ If you smell rotting vegetation, your plants are overwatered.

⇨ If the soil feels dry down to the second knuckle of your index finger, your plants need water.

I know it sounds overly simple, but it isn't when you're out in the garden trying to decide!

Raised Beds

As you start your plans for creating an orna-mental (and edible!) garden, you may want to incorporate raised beds. Don't worry – this isn't as challenging as it sounds. Raised beds are relatively simple to construct and are versatile. If you want to give this garden staple a go, see my construction guide on the next page. And if you're still on the fence, here's a list of reasons why raised beds may be just what your garden needs:

1. **You get to choose your own soil. Some lawns are full of clay soils that rot plant roots before they even get started. Raised beds solve that and other soil problems, like residual chemicals in your yard.**

2. **They make for easier and cleaner work. Depending upon the height of construction, you can sit on the edge, or on a gardening seat and work in comfort.**

3. **Soil inside raised beds stays crumbly and soft, because it isn't walked upon.**

4. **They have the same care instructions as containers. You already know how to grow in containers, and you can main-tain raised beds the same way.**

5. **They can be pretty easily moved if you decide to change up your plan.**

Raised Bed Construction Step by Step

As with anything in gardening, there is no magic formula. You can make raised beds out of many different components, including straw bales, concrete blocks, etc. The only limitation is time, imagination and money. My kitchen garden, which I planned to remain in a permanent location handy to my kitchen, is built out of colored concrete blocks and lined with landscape fabric to stop weeds like Bermuda grass that have deep and extensive root systems. Between you and me, I wouldn't line my blocks all the way to the top with fabric if I had it to build again; I would install the fabric only partway up, because debris gets behind it. However, we learn as we go. That's gardening!

The easiest raised beds I've built are from untreated wood. The following is a simple raised bed we built to extend our garden season.

Note: We built our bed so that it could be covered in winter with a cold frame, for winter growing. Cold frame kits are easy to assemble. Our cold frame's size was 4' x 4', so our bed is the same size. Our raised bed can now serve two functions through the seasons.

Materials

⇨ **WOOD:** Choose wood that is rot resistant and untreated with pesticides. I used Douglas fir for this bed, to maximize its staying power in Oklahoma's dry climate. Some of my raised beds last 10 years or more.

⇨ **FOUR 2" X 12" BOARDS CUT 4 FEET LONG.** Many books suggest 2" x 8" boards, which is fine. For some reason, however, an 8"-wide board actually measures 6½", so if you want to grow root crops like carrots, beets, turnips and potatoes, you may want 2" x 12" to give yourself deeper space for the roots. Hint: Most hardware stores or home improvement centers will cut wood to order if you ask. Some don't even charge.

⇨ **FOUR 1" X 4" CEDAR BOARDS** to screw on the outside of the raised bed, to create a structure on which to place the cold frame later. This isn't necessary unless you plan to convert your raised bed to a cold frame.

⇨ **DECK SCREWS:** I don't like beds made with nails. Period. They come apart over time and cause you grief right when you want to garden. Deck screws, unlike nails and regular wood screws, are weather resistant and drive easier.

⇨ **ELECTRIC DRILL OR SCREWDRIVER:** Borrow, beg or steal – just kidding – an electric drill. Your project will go so much easier than if you use a screwdriver.

⇨ **LANDSCAPE FABRIC (OR HEAVY DUTY WOVEN PLASTIC):** Both of these mediums can present problems. BPA, as discussed on page 6, may expose plants to chemicals; landscape fabric can catch debris and impede growth if you install it to the top of the bed. Instead, install fabric so that it is stapled to the middle of the top board or approximately 2/3 of the way up the bed's side.

⇨ **STAPLE GUN WITH HEAVY-DUTY STAPLES:** While you can nail the landscape fabric in place, it's easier to use a staple gun. If you don't want to buy one, find a handy neighbor who might lend it to you, along with that electric drill.

⇨ **HARDWARE CLOTH (WIRE MESH) AND SCISSORS:** If you live in an area with voles, moles or other burrowing creatures, hardware cloth (wire mesh) will stop them from destroying your garden. If these animals aren't a problem in your region, no need for hardware clotht.

⇨ **DIRT:** I say dirt, but I really mean garden or potting soil mixed with compost. For my raised beds, I've used my own sandy soil mixed with purchased and homemade compost. This wouldn't work as well for clay soils, so if you use your own soil, test it first. You can get soil test kits from your local cooperative extension system office. Local companies sell soil and sometimes compost (any amount from a five-gallon bucket to a dump-truck load).

If you buy, ask plenty of questions. Garden-ready soil should already have compost mixed throughout. It is the Cadillac of soil, but talk to them about what goes into it. You are growing vegetables – nutrient hogs – in a small place, so you'll need fertile, balanced soil.

A note on soil: If you don't have a place to buy soil locally, you can purchase good quality potting soil and mix it with different kinds of compost, purchased or homemade. Add composted horse, cattle or poultry manure for increased fertility, but watch out for persistent herbicides, as mentioned on page 25. Also, most manure needs to age first, so it won't burn your plants. However, rabbit and goat pellets aren't "hot" and can be added immediately; if you know someone who keeps bunnies, see if you can trade vegetables for bunny poo. Worm castings are good, too.

Assembly

1. Choose a level space in your yard to build and place the bed.

2. Cut hardware cloth and landscape fabric to size. (The one we're building is 4' x 4'.)

3. Lay out the boards and bring their corners together. Using the electric drill with a screw attachment, drive three screws into the joint to hold the boards together. You can pre-drill holes, but it's not necessary if you use deck screws and a screw attachment on your drill.

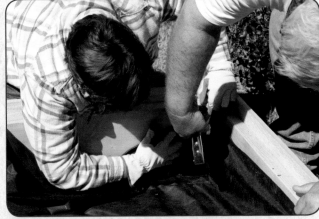

4. Attach the landscape fabric to the interior of the bed with staples, making a lining that goes ²/₃ up the boards. Don't worry if the cloth isn't perfectly straight. It will be covered with soil. At this point you should have a freestanding wooden framework with the bottom lined with landscape fabric.

5. (Skip this step if you don't need to deter burrowing creatures.) Turn over the bed and staple the hardware cloth to the bottom of the boards. This wire mesh should be beneath your landscape fabric and, when the bed is in place, between it and the ground.

6. Place the bed where you want it to stay. You could anchor the bed with pieces of rebar on the outside of boards for stability, but once soil is placed inside, we've never had stability problems.

7. Fill your bed with soil and water until moist.

Now you're ready to plant!

Situate raised beds in a sunny spot near your house. Use as much of your yard as you'd like – but again, start small. You can always add as your garden vision grows.

Not a DIY'er?
Ready-Made Raised Beds

If you want the ease of raised beds, but you don't want to build them from scratch, you can also purchase a variety of kits, including a Grow Bed in periwinkle or black (see Resources). Grow Beds are made of heavyweight plastic, but you can buy a liner specially designed for them. Installation is easy: snap the four pieces into place and then place the liner inside. Periwinkle Grow Beds are especially cute because they take a standout color and make it the focus of your planting area. Imagine how cool green plants would look against that plummy shade.

Want something even simpler? Smart Pots®, made of a strong and flexible fabric, now have a Big Bag Bed; it's round (50 inches in diameter) and gives you 13½ square feet of growing space; see photo at left. These are the simplest to install because you simply decide where they should go, unfold and fill them with your soil and compost mixture. Later, if you decide to move the bed, just remove the soil, and your garden becomes portable. If you're living in an apartment or rental house, fabric pots would be a great way to grow.

Fresh herbs are delicious and add flavor to any meal. Read on for ideas on what to grow in your raised bed herb garden.

Starting an Herb Garden

Here's the thing about herbs: they are both beautiful and functional. They also grow almost anywhere – in a container, in a dedicated herb garden, in an ornamental garden – and this makes them ideal for gardens of all kinds. The only concern about where to grow them is making sure they're close enough to the house to quickly snip for cooking. If your herbs are nearby, you can run outside and grab some basil and rosemary to spice up any dish. I grow many perennial and annual herbs in my potager. Here are just a few:

Perennial Herbs

⇨ **ROSEMARY:** For years, I believed my rosemary died over the winter because it was too cold. Then, I added a small plant to my raised beds, and I finally figured out what was wrong. Rosemary needs sharp drainage, and the raised beds provide just that. I don't even cover it in winter in my USDA Zone 7a garden. A beautiful variety to grow for herb and blooms is 'Tuscan Blue,' but it's only hardy to 20°F.

⇨ **SAGE:** Hardy to Zones 4 to 7, culinary sage is an easy perennial to grow. Like most herbs, it wants lean soil (low fertility) with sharp drainage.

⇨ **THYME:** I grow creeping thyme and lemon thyme. Both overwinter with no protection.

⇨ **CHIVES:** At the front of the beds, my chive plants create symmetry while supplying a touch of oniony goodness to any meal, including baked potatoes, plus, spring blooms for my salads. They bloom early in the year, giving the vegetable garden color before much else is growing.

Birds are attracted to the seeds of its umbel flowers in late summer. (Umbels are clusters of tiny flowers that grow from a central stem in an umbrella-like form.)

Annual Herbs

⇨ **DILL:** This is a fantastic herb that adds a wealth of flavor. I particularly enjoy it on fish and in potato salad. I would include it in my garden for taste alone, but it has the added benefit of attracting swallowtail butterfly caterpillars.

⇨ **PARSLEY:** It's a slow starter, so while I do scatter some seed, I also buy one plant in the spring to get a head start. I prefer Italian parsley (the flat-leafed kind), but curly varieties are also good. While parsley does overwinter in my garden, it soon bolts at the first sign of heat, so I consider it an annual.

⇨ **BASIL:** This is my favorite herb, hands-down. With its vibrant, summery flavor and variety of cultivar choices, how could it not be? 'Genovese' is a heavily-perfumed Italian basil, while 'Siam Queen' and 'Sweet Thai' are much spicier. 'Dark Purple,' 'Purple Ruffles' and 'Dark Opal' have lovely, purple foliage that adds depth to any garden. You owe it to yourself to sample seed catalogs for other interesting basils. They are all delish and easy to grow from seed.

Flowering Herbs (pretty and edible, too!)

Most herbs bloom, but their flowers are often ignored by cooks in favor of their culinary usefulness. Some herbs, however, are grown primarily for their flowers. They fall into the edible flower group more often than their other herb friends. Below are some of the prettiest flowering herbs:

⇨ **CALENDULA:** Plant the seeds early, mid-February in my climate. It takes several seasons to grow to bloom size, but the melon- and peach-colored flowers are worth the wait.

⇨ **BORAGE:** For blue color in the vegetable and herb garden, you can't beat borage. It also self-seeds, so once you plant it, you'll have it for as long as you like. The flowers themselves have a light cucumber taste.

⇨ **LAVENDER:** Nearly everyone loves lavender, but I found it hard to grow, in spite of giving it full sun and good drainage. Then, a gardening friend told me to place a bit of chicken grit or gravel at the bottom of the planting hole, and my lavender has thrived ever since. 'Munstead' is a variety that works well in many places, and 'Hidcote' is a classic.

After experimenting with some of these varieties, you may discover other flowering herbs to enjoy. Just remember not to eat anything in the ornamental garden unless you're sure it's an incredible edible.

Flowers in the Vegetable Garden?

Why plant flowers in the vegetable garden? Because the traditional segmentation
rules of gardening are outdated. Ever since
Rosalind Creasy's books on edible landscaping broke the dividing line between veggies and flowers, there's been a sea change
about what goes where. These two groups of
plants are no longer separated as edible and
non-edible in the landscape. Tasty blooms
and flowering vegetables now find a home in
one, integrated garden plot as long as you
give plants plenty of room in the right location. Look to seed packets and plant tags for
specific information about placement, size
and shape.

Eat lavender, roses and so much more...

There are many flowers that make lovely additions to both the
garden and the dinner table. For flowers that are also edible, these
are my personal favorites: rose petals, lavender, pansies and violas,
nasturtiums, borage, chives and calendulas. Old roses often have
terrific fragrance and make nice additions to baked goods, vinegars,
jellies and mixed drinks. Nasturtiums are a little bit spicy and are
lovely atop salads. Borage blooms taste like cucumbers, and chives
like the alliums they are. I find I like most of my floral food items
sprinkled as petals instead of the whole flower. This is especially
true with larger blooms, which can be cumbersome and a little
weird to eat. Always choose organically grown flowers for eating. If
you grow them yourself, you can be sure they're pesticide free.

You can also eat any of the blooms from vegetable plants like
herbs, beans and squash. A general rule to follow is that, if the fruit of the plant is edible, so are the blossoms.
Be a little adventurous and see what you discover. You may find that you love stuffed squash blossoms. My family certainly does. Some people even eat daylilies, but check online before eating the blooms of other plants. You
want to make sure they're not poisonous.

My Top 10 List of Beautiful Edibles

Along with beautiful flowers, there's been an explosion of gorgeous vegetables in recent years. Gone are plain-Jane green beans, to be replaced with speckled (and even purple!) varieties in both runner and bush bean style. Below are my favorite beauty queen vegetables to delight both the eye and your taste buds.

⇨ **RUNNER BEANS:** 'Purple Podded Pole Bean' is a Missouri heirloom. It's a beautiful runner bean, meaning it grows upon a structure instead of low to the ground, and the beans are delicious.

⇨ **BEETS:** 'Bull's Blood' beet is another heirloom, this time from 1840. I grow this one primarily for its deep burgundy foliage, but I also eat the beets when they're small. Both the fruit and greens are excellent.

⇨ **EGGPLANT:** 'Rosa Bianca' eggplants are striped with a blend of pinkish purple and white. Harvest as small fruits – beautiful and tasty.

⇨ **LETTUCE:** 'Redina' French red-leaf lettuce is so attractive that you may not want to eat it, but leaf lettuces, no matter what the color, are great additions to your garden and taste better than anything you buy from the store. Darker leaves also contain extra vitamins.

⇨ **KALE:** 'Lacinato' kale is still in the greens category, but its leaves are a dusky blue/green. It is tender when small and works well in winter and spring soups. It's especially sweet after a cold snap.

⇨ **SWEET PEPPERS:** 'Bullnose' sweet peppers ripen to a deep red. Their fruit is short and stout, with thick walls. A version of 'Bullnose' was grown by Thomas Jefferson, although cross-pollination changes heirlooms over time, and the ones grown today are considerably larger.

⇨ **CAYENNE PEPPERS:** 'Long Red Slim' cayenne peppers stand out in the garden like a stoplight. Although I grow several ornamental peppers just for looks, I think chile peppers, especially cayenne types, are hot in both looks and taste.

⇨ **SAGE:** Culinary sage, either solid or tricolor, is one of the prettiest perennials in the garden. It can be grown almost anywhere with sun.

⇨ **FAVA BEANS:** Fava beans are lovely because of their black and white blooms. Try 'Agua Dulce' and 'Broad Windsor'. They like cool weather, so I'm growing some over the winter to see if I can get an early crop. If the temperature goes down to 32F (and it often does) I'll cover them.

⇨ **SWISS CHARD:** 'Rhubarb' red Swiss chard is the last on my list of beautiful edibles. I've grown all of the popular colors, including pink, yellow and white, but I love the ruby red ones best. Perhaps, you'd rather grow yours hot pink. If so, choose 'Pink Passion' for a surprising burst of color.

What's that ugly plant, and why are you growing it?

Don't be tempted by just a pretty face. What some plants lack in beauty, they make up for in interest or flavor. 'Lumpy Red' tomatoes, for example, are weirdly shaped, with each one looking odder than the next. They have such thin skin that they can't be transported much further than from the garden to your kitchen so you'll never see one in stores. When you cut into them, however, they burst open with a flavor so unique you'll think you've been transported to Shangri-La. 'Jade Sweet' eggplant is another variety you wouldn't see featured on grocery store shelves. Its pale lime-green and blocky fruit wouldn't win a prize for beauty, but the taste and longevity in the refrigerator makes it worthwhile. Keep these unusual plants in mind when choosing between varieties. That odd-looking plant in the corner may just yield your garden's most interesting or tastiest fruit. (*Note:* The yellow tomato in this photo is another tasty, ugly beauty, but its tag was lost before I could record its name. That happens sometimes, despite our best efforts.)

*   *   *

Way to go!

You've mapped out your design and planted your herbs, edible flowers and vegetables. Now, you weed and wait for your harvest to bring you the delicious fruits of your labor. Keep tabs on which strategies worked and which fell short, but don't worry about any mistakes you may make. This book is full of suggestions and strategies, but it's also about putting those into practice and learning what works for you in your environment. Next year, we'll build on your accomplishments, fix any problems you encounter, and continue developing your ornamental, edible garden into a landscape you'll treasure.

Chapter Five

Keeping Small and In Charge

Now that you know about the versatility and simplicity of gardening with raised beds, you can expand the possibilities. As we start to think about year two, we'll look at garden design as a whole, how to keep it small but interesting, including adding ornamental plants and trees and paths - and "gardening up" with vertical plantings. You'll learn a simple way to save seeds, find out more about tomatoes, crop rotation... and which fruits and veggies will overwinter, extending the seasonal beauty of your garden.

Remember the old saying, "Large and in charge?" Maybe that's true in sports like bodybuilding or football, but in gardening, staying small is where you give yourself the best chance to build upon success. Even if you grew tons of tomatoes in your raised beds last year, don't overdo it. Gardeners have a tendency to want to plow more land or construct ever more beds and borders. How do I know this? Well, I garden over an acre at present – alone. That's too much for one red dirt girl to handle, but I still find myself dreaming of new areas to conquer, new plants to try.

Don't stay the same, just don't overdo. That's all I'm saying. Some years, the climate is perfect. Gentle breezes touch your cheek as you drop seeds into little holes and tuck them in. Rain falls, the sun shines, and all is well. Other years see tough drought, and all you harvest are rocks for stone soup. Planting within your ability ensures you'll be ready for whatever comes your way.

Things to Consider Before Planning Your "Small and in Charge" Garden

How small is small? Get a sense of your own limits, both in time and energy. Want to build more raised beds? (I know you want to!) Fine, but keep in mind the watering needs and watering system that will be required. There is room for expansion in the garden plan on the next page. Here, I've drawn an expanded vegetable and fruit garden. If your back or front yard has the space, you can add more beds around the edges. Don't forget paths. The paths in my garden are wide enough for me to pull a garden cart or wheelbarrow through, about 48 inches. That's about the same size you'll need for two average people to walk side-by-side.

A Backyard Garden

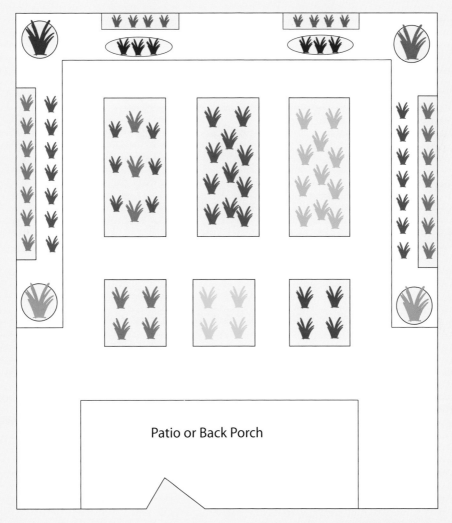

Patio or Back Porch

Note: *I've repeated some of the plants in different beds. This is because you could plant these vegetables in either place. Also, don't forget to rotate your crops to prevent diseases from building up in the soil. You can also substitute pollinator friendly flowers for any vegetable if you wish.*

All of the following are simply suggestions. When more than one plant is listed for a particular bed, pick whichever one you want to grow. The design is color coded to this plant list.

Spring and Fall

⇨ On trellises along both sides of the fence, plant sugar snap peas or snow peas.

⇨ In front of the peas, grow blue kale like 'Toscano.'

⇨ In the back three beds, plant beets, turnips or radishes in the left bed. Around these, fill in with spinach, kale or lettuce. In the middle bed, you can also plant spinach, kale, lettuce or other spring greens. In the right bed, plan turnips or fava beans.

⇨ In the front three beds, plant beets, turnips or radishes in the bed on the left; spring onions in the middle bed; and carrots in the right bed.

Permanent Fruiting Plants

⇨ Small plum tree in the left-hand corner and small peach tree in the right-hand corner.

⇨ Dwarf apple or pear trees along the back fence. (If you would like to try an artistic pruning technique, called espalier, see how on page 87.)

⇨ Fig trees, in front of the apple or pear trees. You could also just plant flowers here instead and save the fig trees for later.

⇨ Strawberries in the two front corners of the borders where the snap peas are.

Summer

⇨ Sow seed for pole beans or cucumbers where you had your snap peas or snow peas before.

⇨ Where you were growing kale in front of the snap peas, now try annual herbs like basil, borage or parsley.

⇨ Replace beets, turnips or radishes with tomatoes. Surround them with basil or hot or mild peppers. In the long center bed, plant bush beans. They produce faster than pole beans so you can have green beans throughout summer. In the long bed on the right, plant sweet corn in a block with the plants alternating as shown for better pollination. You may still need to hand-pollinate these plants though.

For the small beds in front, plant eggplant in the left one, summer squash in the center, and peppers or basil in the right one if your carrots are finished. Carrots take longer to mature.

I placed three 4' x 8' and three 4' by 4' raised beds in the center of the backyard with 4' paths in between. Think about growing crops for at least three seasons of the year, and using cold frames to extend your growing season even further.

You can expand this plan for a larger backyard by adding beds, or a smaller one by subtracting them. I included two small fruit trees in the two back corners of the yard, a plum and a peach. Don't plant them too close to the fence, and ask questions before you buy. These trees are in a small space and require a very dwarf rootstock.

If you've grown a fruit tree successfully in a pot, you can also grow it in a small raised bed or border. All fruit trees grown in containers need significant pruning to keep them small and contained.

Think beyond the season. Most magazines and books photograph vegetable gardens at mid-spring or at the beginning of summer, when plants are beautiful and thriving. This is because most vegetable plants are annuals, and their beauty doesn't last all that long. They work hard to produce their fruit, and once they've been harvested all summer they begin to look ratty. Definitely not photogenic! At that time, you will need to pull them and replant with other veggies, a cover crop, or flowers for your table. I often replace early spring veggies with my summer producing crop. At the end of the season, when I'm thinking about crop rotation, I may leave a bed fallow (empty) and top it off with manure or compost. That way, it's ready for next year.

TIP: Make a sun map, noting how the sun comes up over the garden and how many hours of sunlight it gets during the day. You need at least six to eight hours of sun to grow vegetables well.

As you envision the garden as a whole, beyond the edible plants, it's a good idea to think about adding other interesting plants in your backyard, especially shrubs and trees. Both add structure to the garden that ephemeral vegetables lack. Note: Evergreens, if you can grow them where you live, give year-round interest.

Customize your edibles. In Garden 1, I said that you don't need to grow everything, and that you should grow what you like best to eat. Let's now play with that thought. Grow what's expensive to buy and not readily available at your grocery store or farmers' market. By now, you have the gardening chops to know what you like to eat fresh and how much you can store (whether frozen, dried or canned). Experiment with new varieties you really like but can't find locally, or ones that are grown elsewhere and shipped across the nation unripe – peaches and plums, for example.

Go vertical with trellises and arbors.
One way to increase yield without taking up more land is to grow vines, squash and other space hogs up a trellis or arbor. But keep in mind that annuals don't look beautiful all year, so if you love the way that squash vine looks on the trellis, remember its days of beauty are numbered. My garden has several arbors, including one over the entry, and over the years they've held roses and perennial vines. Flowers smell good and attract pollinators.

Style. When looking for flowers or more building materials, consider the color and style of your home. Is it formal, red brick, or more casual? The type of house and its construction materials can influence the formality of your landscape. My house, for example, is a log cabin and much less formal than a home of brick or stone. Over the years, I've surrounded my home with gardens leaning toward English cottage style, a mix of blowsy flowers, fruit and vegetables.

Formal designs, on the other hand, incorporate straight lines and classic materials like stone, concrete, brick or wood. Raised beds are usually rectangular or square because this is the easiest way to build them. You can create gentle curves with curved concrete blocks or metal edging. Curves do lend a bit of mystery to a garden space because your visitors can't see everything up front and center, but they take more thought and planning.

Paths. Paths in a garden do a number of things. As a design element, they delineate and define your space. Paths also create a clean area to walk upon and keep heavy feet out of your garden beds. Since vegetables tend to look overgrown and messy by midsummer, your garden will appear tidier, no matter the state of your veggies, if you have the same type of raised beds and pathway materials throughout.

What will you use to construct your paths? They can be constructed out of almost anything, including straw for a classic vegetable garden path, decomposed granite or brick (pricey, but beautiful), bark or even grass clip-pings. You can also leave grass in place. I did for years. Be careful of the type of grass, though. Bermuda grass with its underground lateral roots will encroach upon your beds. Straw is preferable to hay, which still has seed heads in it that can sprout, making paths messy.

Note: Some communities require paths to be perme-able so that rainwater can penetrate and drain through path materials and into the ground. This replenishes groundwater and prevents so much water from going directly into storm drains. It's a good thing to know about. Check local ordinances and online for further information.

Forget perfection. Now, I don't want to give you the impression that I'm telling you what to do. If you want to mix up your raised beds, borders and paths, go ahead and construct them from a variety of materials, like straw bales, concrete blocks, brick, or even recycled materials (to be found on freecycle.org). It's your garden. I tire of gardening experts who speak of secret formulas and the "right" way of doing things. Here's the secret . . . there is no secret. Gardening just involves consistent work in a space, doing things like planting, tying up and harvesting. It's as simple as that. As for building a garden, these are some design principles I'm presenting. While they do bring harmony to a space, I never want perfectionism to hinder you.

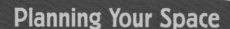

Planning Your Space

Gardening takes some planning. If you've added more raised beds, you will need to decide where you want them and what to plant in them. Start your planning in late January or early February, when the holiday season is over and you're bored with winter. I do some of my best thinking around this time. After Valentine's Day, I'm stir-crazy, wanting to get my hands in the dirt. I manage to ward off late winter blues by planning and re-planning my garden.

I don't know how graphic you want to get, but if you'd like to start imagining the logistics of the space, you can draw a simple design for your beds with graph paper and colored pencils. You can also create a down-and-dirty columned table on your computer.

Biointensive gardening

Biointensive gardening (growing plants close together in a small space) is especially popular in urban areas where sunlight and planting area are premium commodities. One type of biointensive gardening is square foot gardening, a style and term coined by Mel Bartholomew. It uses 4' x 4' square beds, like the one we built in the previous chapter. You would then divide your beds into sixteen squares of planting space. Each square foot is devoted to a particular plant, but the number of plants depends upon how much room a plant needs for growth

and harvest. For example, you can plant four lettuce plants per square foot, or, for larger plants like tomatoes and summer squash, one plant per square foot. While some of the details of square foot gardening are too much math and structure for me, I do use some of Bartholomew's intensive growing practices, like close plant spacing, rich compost, and loose, friable soil. There are entire communities devoted to square foot gardening online, and many participants create charts showing the best planting schemes. Bartholomew also has a website if you need more information.

Block planting. I grow intensively (meaning I try to harvest the most produce in a small space with less water) with a method called block planting. Gone are long, straight rows of vegetables; in their place are blocks of productive plants. Larger crops, like tomatoes and squash, take up half of a four-foot bed, while other tidier crops, like peppers, are planted one foot apart.

My Smelly Recipe for Manure Tea

What you'll need:

- ○ 5-gallon plastic container with lid or weighted top
- ○ ¼-½ yard of natural muslin or other strong cotton fabric
- ○ 2-4 cups of chicken manure
- ○ Water
- ○ String
- ○ Small weight with a hole in the middle (for the string)

What to do:

1. Cut muslin into a square and place it on a flat surface. Scoop chicken manure onto the square and bring the ends of the fabric together. Tie off the ends and cut the string long enough to hang outside of the bucket. Tie a weight at the end of the string to keep it from falling into the water. (You won't want to be fishing around in the manure tea to grab the bag!)

2. Place the bag of manure into the bucket and fill the bucket with water. Cover the bucket and leave it to sit somewhere outside for a period of a week to three weeks.

3. Check it periodically and stir the water with the bag of manure. After brewing, the concoction will smell, but plants love it. It will be the consistency and color of tea. You can top off the bucket with more water as summer progresses, or you can redo the entire process.

Use manure tea to feed plants weekly in the summer months. It makes a good foliar fertilizer or soil drench, and plants respond to your care.

If you don't want to make your own manure tea, buy it from Annie Haven – http://www.manuretea.com/. It's completely organic and doesn't contain persistent herbicides.

More About Tomatoes

TIP: **Saving tomato seeds.**
It is easier to save seeds from tomatoes if you first ferment them. The seeds will separate more readily from the fruit, and the fermentation process stops a natural germination inhibitor. Cut the tomato in half, scoop out seeds and gel. Add water to the gel and seeds and set your container in the shade. After three or four days, a moldy film will probably grow on top. Remove this and pour out seeds. Run water over them again in a cup and dispose of any seed that floats to the top, because the good seeds will sink to the bottom. Drain seeds on a paper towel and leave to dry. Once seeds are dry, store like any other.

Determinate vs. Indeterminate Tomatoes

There are two main categories of tomatoes, determinate and indeterminate. The terms refer to a tomato's growth habits and the timing of their tomato yield. Which should you grow? It all depends on when you want your tomatoes, how many and how much room you have. Let me give you some guidance so you'll know which type of tomato will work for your needs.

Determinate. Determinate tomatoes are often called bush tomatoes because their growth habit is smaller and shorter, and they don't keep on growing throughout the season. Once fruit sets on the bloom, the plants stop growing. They will grow to three or four feet high and wide – unless they are one of the newer hybrids selected specifically for containers or patio gardens. Determinate tomatoes yield most of their crop all at the same time; it takes two to three weeks for a crop to mature. Once your plant produces this crop it begins to weaken. Determinate tomatoes are good for canning or freezing, because your entire harvest will yield at nearly the same time. The good thing about these is that you can count on having the yield you need at the time you need it. Commercial tomato cages that you see in nearly every hardware store work great with determinate tomatoes.

Because the plants stay smaller and bushier, they work best in containers and smaller gardens. Hybrid tomatoes tend to be determinate. Early-bearing varieties like 'Early Girl' are most often determinate. 'Clear Pink Early' is a determinate heirloom variety from Russia.

Indeterminate. Indeterminate tomatoes keep growing and producing throughout the garden season until frost, as long as plants are staked and the sun continues to shine. You will need to stake them or build a heavier tomato cage (often out of wire fencing) to keep indeterminate tomatoes upright, because they will become very heavy. Indeterminate tomatoes should be pruned by removing at least some suckers from the main stem of the plant.

Suckers are stems that grow in the "V" where the main stem attaches to a lateral stem. You can either cut these or pinch them when small and tender. It won't hurt the plant. Living in a hot climate, I do leave a few of these suckers to shade the fruit, preventing sunscald.

You can grow indeterminate tomatoes in large pots, but you will need to stake the entire plant well and provide ballast in the bottom of your pot. Otherwise, plants and even your pot, can blow over and break in the wind. Indeterminate tomatoes grow to six feet or more over the garden season.

Heirloom tomatoes tend to be indeterminate, but not always. While you won't get a crop of tomatoes all at once, you will have fruit throughout the season. Some of my favorite varieties are 'Anna Russian' a.k.a. 'Anna', 'Black Cherry' and 'Cherokee Purple.' All are very dependable in my garden.

Note: There are also **semi-determinate** tomatoes, but you won't see them as often.

Before starting tomato seed or transplanting plants, talk to gardeners in your area. In my opinion, there is no plant more variable and particular to a particular place than the tomato. You'll want to grow the determinate and indeterminate varieties that perform well where you live. People often save tomato seed from heirloom varieties to increase their chances of better yield and disease resistance in their climate. If you can find these selections, you'll be more successful with tomatoes.

Vegetables & Fruit that Overwinter with Ease

While many vegetables are annual or tropical plants, in much of the country others will overwinter. These are the plants that can give your garden more structure. Although many die back to the ground or must be harvested in spring, they do occupy a more permanent place in the garden. Here are some plants to consider:

⇨ **GARLIC:** Hard neck vs. soft neck? I get this question a lot. If you've never grown garlic, you're probably only familiar with soft neck, as it's the type most often found in grocery stores. This is partly due to softneck garlic being easier to store and transport. It also lasts longer in storage. However, if you're going to grow your own, you can pick the type you like. Hardneck garlics are often much more intense and complex in flavor, so foodies love them. Plus, they are easier to peel. Softneck garlics are often recommended for warmer climates, but I've grown both hardneck and softneck successfully. If you live in a colder region, you may want to consider hardneck first.

⇨ **ARTICHOKES:** These statuesque plants are actually perennial in southern states and California. The warm season isn't long enough, unfortunately, for them to fruit and flower in northern states.

⇨ **HORSERADISH:** Horseradish needs a winter cooling period in order to become dormant for harvest. It does spread, so remove all but two roots after harvest. You'll see it again next season.

⇨ **ASPARAGUS:** Asparagus is easy to grow, but it's a time commitment – meaning you have to wait a while for your first crop, but after that it will just keep on coming back, year after year. Place it in a spot where it can grow for 20 years. Seriously...I mean that. Start with a dozen crowns and you'll be harvesting tender spears in two years. There is nothing like homegrown asparagus.

⇨ **RHUBARB:** This is a perennial member of the buckwheat family; it likes cool weather and full sun. If you try it in the South, it requires afternoon shade. Look for newer selections like 'Valentine.' 'Giant Cherry' is reportedly better in warmer areas or those with short winters.

⇨ **HERBS:** Many herbs – including rosemary, fennel, oregano, garlic chives, regular chives, thyme, lemon thyme and sage – will overwinter. Some herbs are especially useful to tumble over walls or large rocks and are as pretty as any trailing plant. *Note:* garlic chives are a nuisance plant in Oklahoma. They spread everywhere.

⇨ **FRUITS:** Many fruits – including strawberries, raspberries and blueberries – overwinter and are, in fact, perennials. In place of regular shrubs in your landscape, try planting blueberries (if you have acidic soil) or raspberries. You'll get structure and delicious fruit. It's a two-fer!

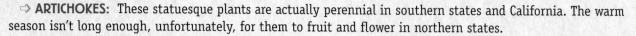

Fabric in the Garden? Oh yes.

Here are three types of cloth that help you garden more efficiently and protect your plants.

⇨ **SHADE CLOTH:** In some parts of the country, the summer sun is just too much for most fruits and vegetables. When you consider that summer vegetables grow best in daytime temperatures between 70°F and 80°F degrees, you see why some years would be hard on plants. Tomatoes get sunscald, a hard whitish patch on one side of the fruit that is ugly and tough. Other plants quit producing, and may even die from overexposure. Where I live, in July and August temperatures can reach 100F degrees or even higher for days on end. So, gardeners, being smart and adaptive to the current climate, use a layer of dark, shade cloth to keep our veggies cool. Shade cloth is like sunscreen for plants.

Some gardeners in southern states build structures with shade cloth that can be lowered or raised, and southern greenhouses nearly always sport shade cloth as temperatures rise. Although black and dark green is most often seen, you can get shade cloth in a variety of dark colors – some with aluminum even woven in for its reflective qualities. Shade cloth comes in a variety of shade percentages too, anywhere from 22% to 90%. Note that 22% isn't going to help your vegetables plants much, and 90% is too much because you need some sun for plants to grow. For the right percentage in your area, check with local garden forums and nurseries. Here, we use greater than 50%, but we also remove shade cloth at night and in the early morning to capture milder rays.

⇨ **FROST CLOTH:** Like shade cloth, frost cloth comes in a variety of sizes. However, that's where their similarities end. Frost cloth is white to absorb the sun in fall and even winter. In addition to frost cloth, plastic should be mentioned because it is also sometimes attached to hoops to protect plants. How well plants will be protected depends upon several factors: the thickness of the cloth or plastic, whether your part of the country has snow cover (snow insulates the areas it surrounds, like an igloo), and how low temperatures go. Thicker frost cloth lets in less sunlight but keeps plants warmer. Check out your local cooperative extension service for the stats in your area.

⇨ **LIGHTWEIGHT ROW COVERS:** This type of nearly see-through white cloth is often used to protect plants from insects that land and feed upon young plants. They can also sometimes discourage deer and birds, although nothing much stops a hungry deer. This cloth is especially effective against squash bugs – a difficult insect to control – if the cloth is anchored properly. I garden in an area with high winds and I anchor my row covers and other garden cloths in a variety of ways, from anchor pins pushed directly into the cloth and soil, to clips and even rocks placed upon the cloth's edge. Some gardeners bury the edge of the cloth in soil, but I find this makes

the cloth dirtier for storage later. I've also seen where other gardeners nail or staple a 1 x 2 board as a weight along the edges of their row covers to hold them in place. You can use clips and wire to attach the cloths to PVC hoops, tying the ends of the shade cloth at the end of each row or section.

You can buy all of these different types of row covers at most hardware and garden stores, or order them online. They come in multiple lengths and widths; but for smaller gardens, simply buy a roll or two to drape over garden structures, like your tomato cages, or PVC (plastic) hoops placed in raised garden beds. If you construct PVC hoops, these same structures can be used to extend the garden season in spring and fall with frost cloth. You can also drape row covers over rebar stakes in your containers or raised beds if you don't want to construct hoops.

Buy the best you can afford. Good quality frost and shade cloth can be used for several seasons, and you don't want to buy cheaply made cloth that tears in its first season and then ends up a landfill somewhere.

Way to go!

So, now that you've grown a second year in your small garden of plenty, I hope you've tried a few of the tips in this chapter. Maybe you built more raised beds and learned about gardening vertically with trellises and arbors. Perhaps, you've branched out into square foot gardening and are learning its methods. Or you've added structure to your garden with trees and shrubs, especially those that bear fruit. Maybe you're now also growing and adding herbs to your dinnertime routine.

I hope you had a sweet harvest. Once vegetables grow to maturity, don't be afraid to try and save some of their seeds. It's not a hard process. Otherwise, people wouldn't have been doing it for millennia. Hybrids are relatively new; if our ancestors hadn't saved seeds, we wouldn't even be here. Give it a try. Even if you don't succeed the first time or two, you will learn something new each time, and one day, you will grow a harvest of plenty from your own seed.

In the next chapter, we'll talk a lot about patience with plants and their growth cycles, along with what may be eating them. I'll show you how to deter the creatures and people who want your bounty as much as you. And introduce you to the pleasures of planting natives, including beautiful wildflowers.

Chapter Six

Stay the Course, but Try Something New

This is where I help you remember to be patient with yourself and the garden. I'll introduce you to some interesting, recent varieties of plants, and then show you a beautiful and space-saving technique for fruit trees and grape vines - all in the interests of enhancing your maturing small garden. I'll also help you identify who's eating your plants and how to deter them - marauding critters, I mean - as well as how to keep human critters from turning your front yard veggie patch into the neighborhood supermarket.

BEFORE WE LOOK AT ALL THE EXCITING THINGS YOU CAN DO IN YOUR GARDEN THIS YEAR, I want to give you a word of encouragement about what you've done so far. Remember those trees, shrubs and perennials you added in the first and second year of the garden? Do they look like they're just sitting there doing nothing?

There's an old garden adage about perennials called *sleep, creep and leap.* The first year you plant anything other than an annual or tropical plant, it can look like Sleeping Beauty in her bedchamber. But looks can be deceiving... your plant was doing a lot of growth below the surface of the soil where you couldn't see it.

Giving perennials a good start. Perennials, and by this, I also mean trees and shrubs, take *at least* the first year to start acclimating themselves to their environment. That's why it's so important to water all plants, but especially perennials, regularly during the first year. They are like babies. They can't fend for themselves yet even if your weather is pretty good. All plants need at least an inch of water a week to thrive. The second year of life, perennials spend growing, but at such a snail's pace it seems like they are creeping. Finally, in the third year, you'll see real growth in leaves and stems – the leaping phase. Trees, because they are the longest-lived plants on Earth, can take even more years to get their growth on. So, be patient with your garden and yourself.

I have to agree with garden writer Anne Wareham's take on things. She says, "Plants want to grow; they are on your side as long as you are reasonably sensible."

In your third year of container gardening, we talked about trying new plants for your containers. I hope you do the same here. Many of the plants we discussed in Garden 1 can also apply to Garden 2. You're just growing them in-ground or in raised beds. Remember that raised beds are just bigger containers.

TIP: In years with a late spring freeze, you probably won't see any fruit on trees and shrubs even though you have good bloom. Try not to get discouraged. In southern states, we are plagued with late freezes. Southerners had to learn to enjoy blooming trees for the pretty things they are, even when we don't get any produce. Each stage of the garden year holds its own joys, but fruiting years are even sweeter.

New plants on the block. While we're trying something new each year, why not experiment with a new or unusual variety of produce? Some of the ones below are even new to me because 2014 is their first year in regular commerce. Gardening never gets old, especially when there's something new to grow.

New or Unique Veggie Varieties and Their Seasons

Variety	Spring/Fall	Summer	Start Indoors/ Sow Outside	Qualities
'Shiraz' snow peas	X		SO	Purple pods when harvested young are tender. They are also high in antioxidants.
'Babybeat' beets	X		SO	Miniature red beet; great for containers and small spaces
'Amethyst Improved' basil		X	Either	Dark purple Genovese type basil is beautiful and holds its color.
'Cosmic Purple' carrots	X		SO	Purple skin with yellow or orange flesh is beautiful
'Cherokee Long Ear' corn		X	SO	Variety selected for popcorn or decoration has multicolored kernels.
'Lady Pea' cowpeas		X	SO	Small and tasty variety; works great in smaller gardens.
'Tadifi' eggplant		X	SI	Small round, purple and white variety originally from Syria.
Red orach	X		SO	Drought and heat tolerant spinach substitute should still be grown in spring and fall.
'Champion Purple Top' rutabagas	X		SO/but may need to start indoors in the South	Mild, sweet rutabagas; so much better than those found in stores.
Lemon summer squash		X	SO	Great resistance to insects
'Mascotte' French green beans		X	SO	This AAS 2014 Vegetable seed winner has small and productive plants that are great for any size gardens including containers. The bean pods are held above the plants for easy picking.

Discover garden cloches

What is a garden cloche? The term is French (meaning bell) and generally refers to a translucent, glass, bell-shaped cover that goes over a small plant to protect it from the cold or hungry animals in spring. It does this by absorbing sunlight during the day and holding onto that warmth from the soil at night. Cloches are like mini-greenhouses for specific spots in the garden. People also use wire and twig cloches to protect their small transplants from hungry animals in early spring.

Although glass cloches are beautiful, they are also pricey...and fragile. One bad hailstorm, or an accidental knock from you, and they're history. So, while I collect glass cloches and occasionally use them outside, like many gardeners, I also make inexpensive ones from two-liter soda bottles. Visit the 20-30 Something Garden Guide blog for my easy how-to.

Something new for fruit tree lovers

If the limited size of your garden has you thinking you can't have fruit trees – and if you have a sturdy wall or a fence – what about trying an Old World technique called *espalier?*

Espalier

Espalier is a French term for a bio-intensive gardening process. Espalier is a beautiful art form because trees are pruned to grow on one level or plane against a wall, fence or structure in your garden. Originally, they were grown on walls to capture the heat radiating from the structure. It is often done with fruit trees, especially pears and apples, but can also be done with grapes and even non-blooming trees. I've seen espaliered evergreens. The fence surrounding your yard would be beautiful adorned with an espaliered tree or two. Espaliered trees are not just beautiful. They also take up less space and tend to be more productive. Pruning trees into a form does require some maintenance, but fruit trees require maintenance anyway. You can buy trees already partially trained and continue to train them yourself, but these trees can be quite expensive.

Where to plant. Start with a small tree planted six to eight inches away from your fence. This would be especially nice at the end of your beds as a permanent focal point. See the drawing at right. If you're growing a tree that needs cross-pollination, like an apple, you may want to start with a tree that has several different varieties of apple grafted on it (see Resources), or more than one tree. Fig trees also make excellent espaliers, and they are easy to prune, blooming on new wood.

Espaliered Pear Tree

Before you prune

Choose your desired shape. Some common shapes (forms) are:

Cordon. This means trained to a single stem. Most espaliers I've seen are trained to a single stem. From there, they can be as complicated or simple in shape as you desire. Some are braided while others look like candlelabras.

Palmette Verrier a.k.a. candelabra. This one is very popular and the style I love best. I'll show you how to do it on the next page, step-by-step. You start with a central stem and train the branches into a u-shaped pattern that resembles a candlestick.

Fence patterns. These are often used by large gardens, like the Chicago Botanic Garden to separate planting areas and to show visitors how to prune. You can also do a fence pattern, but you'll need several trees, and these are much more complicated.

Note that you can also train your espaliered tree into an informal shape. Look online for further patterns. Espalier has seen a resurgence in popularity in recent years so there are plenty of photographs on the Internet. Choose one that suits you.

Pruning

How you train your tree will depend upon the pattern you pick. Do most of your pruning in late winter before your tree breaks dormancy (starts to form buds). Don't worry, new branches are very pliable and easy to bend. In the drawings below, the dotted lines indicate where to make your cuts.

First year: Let buds and branches develop into long shoots and keep your tree watered and healthy.

Second year: Start with one main stem called the leader. Cut it at 15 to 18 inches above the ground leaving three to four buds or branches below the cut. As lateral branches grow, bend them on either side of the vertical leader into horizontal lines. Remove lateral branches that don't conform to your pattern. You'll notice that during the spring and summer, additional branches will form along the horizontal branch and vertical stem. Trim these away as you notice them. It should look like the cross shown above. Tie leader and lateral branches gently to wires and screws you've anchored in the fence or wall.

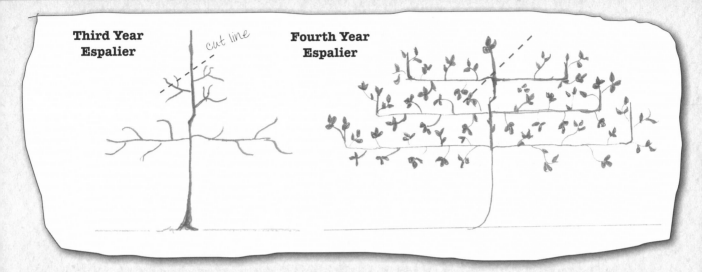

Third year: Cut the leader at or near the spot where you want to begin your second set of lateral branches to grow. The central leader will continue to grow upward with only a slight jog in the stem. You will need to train the second tier of branches the same way you did the first.

Fourth year: Continue to train your espalier until you reach the desired height. Once you've reached this point, cut back the central leader so that the top tier is two lateral shoots. Two or three tiers make a bold statement in the garden. During growing season, leaves and small shoots will fill in part of the pattern some, but always keep your espalier maintained to its desired height and form. Soon, you'll be harvesting fruit from this beautiful tree that is also a piece of living art in every season.

How to Protect Your Garden From Marauding Wildlife

Urban settings didn't used to have the kind of wildlife that they do now. Deer, birds and small mammals like groundhogs, voles and moles were pushed to the edge of civilization. Now, they are coming back in.

Bambi is so much more than a cute and lovable cartoon character from your childhood; he grows up to bamboozle you with his voracious appetite. If you like to eat something in your garden, odds are that every creature in your neighborhood does, too. From the lowly groundhog to cunning raccoons, there are ways to divert them from your garden space. Will you be able to eliminate all damage? No. But you may be able to find a way for you to share a bed of your harvest without giving all of it to the animals in your neighborhood.

Who did that? First, try to identify what is eating your plants or digging them out of the ground. Sounds simple, but this isn't as easy as you may think. Many animals are nocturnal, snacking on our plants at night. This makes it harder to catch Bambi at his game. Be on the lookout for paw prints, and snap a photo of them with your smart phone or camera. Take this to your local extension service or search online and compare. You may quickly discover who your marauder is.

Discouraging Deer and Their Ilk, While Encouraging Other Garden Wildlife

The No. 1 Deterrent. Owning active dogs deters more wild animals than any other method I've used. My fearless canine, Maddie, a rescue from the pound, wants nothing with four legs to roam her yard. Thank goodness she loves people. She and her brother, Tap, always have a warm and dry place to stay in the covered dog run attached to our house. However, they always have access to the outdoors at night. I can do this because I live in the country, where their barking doesn't bother my neighbors. This might not work in a suburban or urban setting, though. Maddie and I spend much of the day outside in the garden where she is always by my side. She

keeps down the vole and mole population, and I've yet to see evidence of a badger anywhere. Squirrels and rabbits know to keep out of her way, too.

Fencing. All of my gardens are fenced. The back garden has split rail fencing, along with field fence that's half buried into the ground to block most burrowing animals. However, the only thing that will stop deer is electric fencing or plastic deer fence (made specifically for that purpose). I live in a state where hunting is still common, and I think that's why we aren't overrun with deer. My husband and I don't hunt, but I'm glad the deer in our neighborhood are skittish of human beings. While I see them now and then at the edges of the property, they want nothing to do with Maddie or me.

Plantings. Another deer preventive measure is to plant large ornamental grasses along the exterior of your garden. I know of one daylily hybridizer who adopted this plan. Deer love daylilies, which are edible to them and us, and will destroy a daylily garden faster than you can say, "Scat!" However, deer don't like the sound of large grasses rustling in the wind or situations where they can't see danger. Try planting a barrier of large, tall grasses in an area that you want to be deer free.

Repellents. Repellents work, but they have to be reapplied frequently. I mostly spray repellents on my fruit trees. Expect a strong smell when you spray, and make sure that you take a shower afterwards. In areas with high deer traffic, repellents may not work as well with uber-hungry deer. Try rotating repellents that have different ingredients to increase effectiveness. I've found the best repellents have rotten eggs in the mixture. (See Resources for various repellents.)

Rabbits. Rabbits occasionally make their way into my back garden, but usually only in spring. Most animals are hungrier just as winter is ending; their fat stores are depleted and there isn't as much wild food available. To protect young plants from rabbit damage, I cover them with chicken wire bent into the shape of inverted bowls. Tall containers also deter rabbits because they can't reach your plants. I've also made willow basket enclosures from the weeping willows on my property. You can turn a basket upside down over a plant that you're trying to save.

TIP: Canned cat food is a great bait to lure many wild creatures into a trap.

Live traps. To trap creatures like gophers and raccoons, purchase a large live trap. Before placing a trap, though, plan for what you will do with the animal once you've captured it. A wild animal in a cage can be dangerous, and they can carry deadly diseases, like rabies. Some cities will come and pick up the animal once you've trapped it, but where I live, we're on our own. We have to relocate them ourselves.

For more information about preventing damage from other unwelcome animals," there's, lots of information online.

Preventing Theft by Two-Legged Bandits

But animals aren't your only problem. In cities and suburban lots, passersby often think it's okay to sample the merchandise. I know friends who have gone out to harvest a tasty tomato from their front yard only to find it missing. People don't always limit themselves to produce, either; they sometimes steal whole plants.

How do we share our urban gardens with friends, neighbors and those less fortunate, while keeping some for ourselves? It's a good question, and some of my friends have come up with great answers:

Jennifer Hammer gardens in California on a small urban lot. One year, she lost all of her tomatoes to people who stole whole plants. Her solution?

○ *Grow tomatoes in the backyard instead of the front.*
○ *Grow lesser-known vegetables in the front yard, like tomatillos, kale, chard, broccolini and herbs.*
○ *Plant mixed borders of attractive vegetables like peppers and chard with flowers.*
○ *Grow taller flowers around the edge of the yard to hide what's growing in the center.*

Tricking thieves doesn't mean you have to be opposed to sharing. "If someone asks for vegetables and flowers I would share," says Jennifer. "I grow plenty."

Jennie Brooks of Oklahoma keeps her vegetables close to her house to prevent theft, since she has loads of foot traffic coming and going from the elementary school nearby. The most trouble she's had is with her small fishpond. "It seems irresistible once kids know it's there." They want to play with the fish, and that's not good for my fish."

Tracy Thatcher, who lives in California, decided to put all of her more exotic edibles (like huckleberries, elderberries, Manzanita, thimbleberries and sorrel) in the front part of her front yard, since people in California aren't as familiar with them. She tucks shorter lettuces and kales beneath taller plants where they aren't as easily seen.

In other words, keep your neighbors close and your plants closer. Being proactive seems the best way to stop people from taking your food and flowers right out from under your nose.

Still, we gardeners are by our very nature a sharing sort, and the beauty of our gardens is also a gift we give freely to others: gardeners like Jennifer Hammer, who would gladly share if someone would ask; and my friend Sandy Yost of North Carolina, who grows wildflowers and picks them with neighborhood children. She takes the time to educate them on what's good to eat and what should be avoided.

Way to go!

Year three in the garden is a special one because you begin to see real progress, and the garden doesn't seem so "new" anymore. Instead, you've become good friends. You know which plants need extra help, and those that fly almost solo. You're also getting to know the creatures who visit the garden regularly. In the next section of the book, Garden 3, we'll focus upon the wonderful creatures – the pollinators and others – that you want to lay out the welcome mat for. Without them, the garden doesn't seem quite as alive, and the plain truth is, you'll get less good food. Garden 3 is all about how to create a pleasure garden for your senses. I can't wait to show you!

Garden 3

A Garden to Delight the Senses

Chapter Seven

Creating a garden of delights

Our first year in Garden 3 finds us planning an environment that engages our senses yet still retains the functionality we need from a small space. This garden is flexible and expandable. We'll be looking at touchable plants, edible plants, fragrant plants, plants that move in the breeze - and I'll tell you about my favorite "sensual flowers."

IF YOU'RE SOMEONE WHO INCORPORATES A YOGA PRACTICE INTO YOUR DAILY ROUTINE, as I do, you've probably discovered that it's more than just exercise – it's a meditation that stretches mind, body and soul. Gardening is no different. There's that moment on a fall day when you're planting lettuce seeds or clipping back an aster. The sun is shining on your hair, and all is right in your world.

Gardening is so much more than harvest. It involves all of our senses. We see our plants and nurture them. We rub the soil between our fingertips. We hear the wind rush scattering leaves around us as seasons change. We smell vegetables and flowers fresh picked. Only after all of this do we taste what we've grown. Gardening is full of such moments if you remain in them and savor their gifts.

Gardening is also a movement. It's a clarion call to step away from the computer and worldly cares. So much information rushes at us every day in our digital world, and we can do so little to change much of it. I don't know about you, but there are days after I've spent so much time working with my computer that I feel numb. Gardening and all it incorporates soothes my soul, stretches my mind and opens my heart. It is more than lifting bags of soil and tucking plants into the ground. It is a way to reconnect with Mother Earth and feel whole again.

Engage your senses

Let's grow a garden that pleases all of our senses, one to delight any child, especially our inner adolescent. Did you have a playhouse when you were little? No? I didn't either, although I always dreamed of one. But I did have a large mimosa tree in my backyard, and I climbed it every day to read a book, listen to birds or take in the sites of my small neighborhood from my grand perch. Whenever I smell the sweet scent of mimosa blossoms – a weed tree to others – I'm drawn back to those carefree moments of sublime comfort nestled in the branches of my tree. Now that I've grown up, my garden is my pleasure palace. It is full of vegetables and fruit to nourish my body and flowers to warm my heart. My inner child feels blessed.

At thirty, I gave birth to my daughter Megan. Bill and I were also raising a teenaged daughter, Ashley, whom I thought of not as my stepdaughter, but as my bonus daughter. Soon, two more babies, Brennan and Claire, followed, and I learned how to garden more efficiently in naptime snippets. Good tools and a timer entered my life as essentials. I still occasionally set my phone's timer when I'm outside. I know, it's breaking my rule about stepping away from tech, but tech isn't the enemy. It's all in how we use it.

I determined to educate my children about the natural world so they wouldn't fear it. Children are so open to nature when they're small, and we can learn from them. Whether you're planning a garden for yourself or the other children in your life, let's make it one full of softness that welcomes you home each day.

Until this point, we've mostly talked about gardening with vegetables. Although I touched earlier upon growing ornamental plants for pollinator-attraction and beauty, it's time to expand on the subject and talk about plants that will give you the gift of sheer delight.

A Garden Plan for the Senses

In this garden sketch, I've chosen nine plants, each with its own kind of sense appeal – for its touchability, taste, color or fragrance...or just for its pleasing, gentle motion in a breeze. Later in the chapter I'll suggest substitutes you could make, but first I want to give you a general feeling for this kind of garden. I can't say it enough times: it's yours to play with and make your own.

Although I made these mounded raised beds curved, feel free to build them in whatever shape you like best. Round shapes in the garden immediately attract attention because they are different. You won't find many straight lines in nature, so adding some curves to your garden brings a sense of harmony.

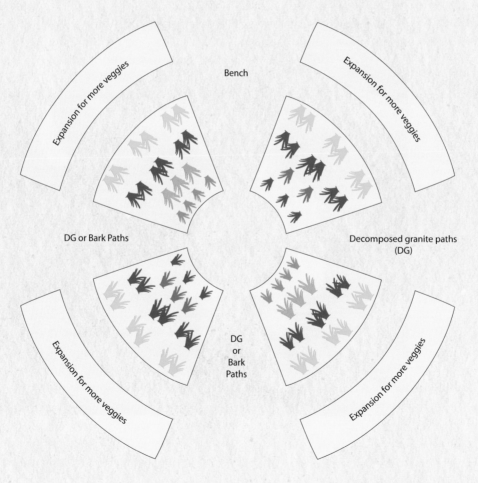

Laying Out the Circle

Before laying out this garden, I would suggest finding the center point in your yard or chosen area and working outward from there. You'll need stakes, landscaper string with chalk, and a level.

To make the circle, start at your center point and use the string and stakes like a compass in math. Once you have marked off your circle with chalk, you can then use it to create your pathways and the first set of surrounding beds. Because this design is more structured than the others in this book, I would probably use decomposed granite or bark in the paths. (I talk more about pathway materials in the next chapter.)

This garden, as all gardens should be, is left open to future expansion and enhancements. Don't plant everything at one time, because with each success, you'll probably want to plant more of whatever worked for you the previous year.

The Plants:

Using the color code in my garden plan, here are the plants for the basic arrangement. I selected them for their ease of care and the many ways they can tickle your senses and give pleasure.

⇨ **LAMB'S EARS:** These silvery, drought resistant perennials are soft to the touch. They are special favorites of children and adults, who like to feel the garden beneath their fingertips. (For more, see Touchable Plants, on page 103.)

⇨ **CREEPING THYME OR LEMON THYME:** Thyme smells good, is great in cooking and makes a small mat of foliage for the front of the garden. If it works in your climate, you can also plant woolly thyme, but in my garden, the drainage has never been good enough for it to last beyond a season or two.

⇨ **FENNEL:** Choose either regular garden fennel or bronze fennel. Both are lovely smelling and good for cooking with. (For more, see Touchable Plants, on page 103.)

A Garden for Memories

In this design I've placed thornier plants like the roses in the center of planting beds, away from small hands. If you want children to smell the roses, you'll need to bring blooms down to their little noses. Mike Shoup, owner of the Antique Rose Emporium, tells a story of a friend who pretended to take his daughter's picture as she smelled rose after rose in his garden.

Little kids love to pose for photos, but he pretended because this was before digital cameras, and film was expensive. His idea was to have her remember him from the roses' scent.

Yes, I've done the same thing with children in my garden. Our olfactory sense is our most primitive and oldest. We retain scent longer than any other memory. To have children who later grow up and remember you from your garden is priceless. What else could you do to make that happen?

⇨ **'HAMELN' OR 'LITTLE BUNNY' GRASSES:** Smaller than switchgrass (listed below), dwarf fountain grasses are wonderful additions to the front or near the front of the border.

⇨ **HEIRLOOM ROSES:** (See the list of scented plants later in the chapter) I am suggesting heirloom or antique roses because many are more highly scented with complex fragrances than modern roses. Because we garden organically, whichever rose you choose should have built-in disease resistance. Also, ask questions at the nursery where you buy your rosebush. Find out if it was sprayed with pesticides or fungicides before you buy. You may be allergic to fungicides and pesticides, especially long-acting ones, which can remain harmful to pollinators and you. It's okay to ask the nursery what sprays they use and when plants were sprayed.

⇨ **SWITCHGRASS:** Plant one on either side of each of the roses. These native grasses are more popular than ever, and you can find a number of great varieties in different color shades from blue gray to yellow. If you want height, use one like 'Northwind.' The sound of grasses blowing in a breeze is soothing to the spirit. They also turn beautiful colors in the fall.

⇨ **SUNFLOWERS:** I love sunflowers in all shapes and sizes. Here, because they are at the back of the border, I would use taller ones in different shades. You can order seeds and sow them directly into the ground. Protect small seedlings from birds that love to eat them by covering with netting or a garden cloche when they first emerge. Soon, they will be tough, and birds will wait for their seeds.

⇨ **CORN:** If you'd rather plant corn along the back of the beds, it would look great too. You will probably need to hand pollinate it because the plants may not be close enough together for the wind to pollinate your corn for you. Here's how to do it: As you walk through the garden, gently shake the stalks to release pollen from the tassels (top of the corn plant) so it falls onto the silks (top of the ears). You can also run your hand gently across the tassels to release the pollen. You'll know to do this when the tassels have pollen hanging from them, and silks on the ears have formed. Hand pollination almost feels like magic to me, whether I'm pollinating squash or corn.

⇨ **RUNNER BEANS:** You can have some fun with these because they love to climb on taller plants. Plant seeds at the base of either the sunflowers or corn when plants are about two feet high. Some people plant seeds for corn/sunflowers at the same time as the beans, but I've found in my garden that the beans grow faster than the plant they're supposed to climb upon.

If you want to create a three sisters planting (see Glossary), you can also plant vines for winter squash or melons beneath sunflowers/corn. Or, if you don't mind things being a little messy, you can let the squash or melon vines trail throughout the rest of the garden.

Touchable Plants

My youngest daughter attended middle school at a small school without resources for landscaping or a gardener. I stepped in, transplanting favorite, kid-friendly plants from my own garden. Between the building and sidewalk I placed soft grasses like 'Hameln' and 'Little Bunny,' along with fuzzy, silvery lamb's ears and highly scented flowers like dianthus (pinks) and pansies. One day, while deadheading the roses at the back of the bed, I saw a small boy bend down to touch the lamb's ears. Soon, he toddled over to the grasses, running his hand through them as he walked. His father gave me an apologetic look and told him to stop. I smiled and said it was "okay to touch" in this garden. With that small border, I had touched the life of at least that one student. I wonder how many others were touched, and I didn't even know.

When planning your own garden, don't forget to add touchable plants. Here are some to get you started; some are edible, but not all. Note: Some grasses and other ornamental plants can be invasive depending on where you live, so check with local sources before you dig.

⇨ **FENNEL:** (listed in my garden plan) Try bronze fennel or the green bulbing type, also called Florence fennel. Both are edible and beloved by butterfly caterpillars and other pollinators. Brush your fingers along fennel's fronds, and you'll probably catch a slight scent of anise or licorice. Even if you're not a licorice fan, you may still love fennel because the flavor is subtle. I use bronze fennel as a salad garnish, and eat green fennel bulbs grated in salads, roasted and grilled. Once you have fennel in your garden, you will always have it because it reseeds with abandon. Even if you collect seeds for eating, you can't catch them all. Fennel is very soft to the touch and a wonderful addition to any garden, whether it's utilitarian or completely ornamental.

⇨ **CARROTS:** Yummy and sweet, raw or cooked, the tops are also beautiful and soft to the touch. While your carrot roots grow beneath the soil, their tops are pretty and tactile above ground, too.

⇨ **ASPARAGUS:** A delicious and long-lived perennial vegetable in any garden, asparagus is also quite attractive once its stems grow into fern-like foliage. This soft effect makes asparagus an excellent backdrop for other plants. While you'll relish young and emerging asparagus shoots, wait a couple of years as asparagus puts its energy into creating a sturdy root system.

⇨ **MINT:** Spearmint, peppermint and chocolate mint all feel good and smell nice. Mints can be quite invasive, so plant them in containers instead of directly in the ground. You can place containers in an ornamental garden if you want. Just make sure you can water them easily. I love spearmint and chocolate mint.

⇨ **SCENTED GERANIUMS:** Fuzzy leaves in multiple shades of green and scented with lemon, spice, rose and other fruits, these gorgeous plants deserve their place in a touchable border. You can overwinter scented geraniums by bringing them inside.

Some purely ornamental touchables

⇨ **LAMB'S EAR:** (listed in my garden plan) While it's used as a medicinal herb, I wouldn't ever eat lamb's ear. All those fuzzy leaves also make deer leave it alone. Probably the favorite plant of most children, lamb's ears are grown primarily for their soft, fuzzy leaves of silvery gray. The soft hairs and gray color also let you know they're extremely drought resistant.

⇨ **ORNAMENTAL GRASSES:** Most ornamental grasses are very soft and pliable with medium to large seed heads beginning mid-summer and often climaxing in fall. Fountain grasses, with their waterfall form that reminds me of Cousin It from the Addams Family, are especially touchable. It's hard to resist giving them a pat as you walk by. 'Fireworks' purple fountain grass is a small grass with large impact.

⇨ **DUSTY MILLER:** Another gray and fuzzy plant with touchable leaves, its short stature makes it a given for the front of the border. It's also just the right size to bend down and touch it.

⇨ **WORMWOOD (ARTEMISIA):** There are several plants in this genus that are great, from short 'Silver Mound' to large 'Silver King.' I really like 'Powis Castle' because of its delicate leaves.

Grow plants that move in the breeze

Grasses and other plants with fern-like leaves are the first to move in a soft breeze. Their foliage also plays with sunlight, making patterns on pathways and other plants. They show, in an immediate sense, how the garden isn't static, but instead, always changing.

Along with scent and touch, we have the benefit of seeing so much more if we take our time. Color is the first thing anyone notices in a garden, but gardeners don't live by color alone. To plan a sensory garden, consider color, texture and form. Varying leaf shape, size and texture makes a more interesting garden palette. Vegetables, fruit, foliage and flowers add up to a whole much greater than their individual parts.

Inspiration for the Planting Beds and Beyond

Trees and shrubs

I encourage you to plant shrubs and trees, including those fruit trees we saw in Garden 1's third year. If you're planning a garden for your senses, dwarf conifers and other evergreens make great accents in the garden year round. My dry and hot climate has few native evergreens so I plant those I truly love in sheltered places where they thrive.

Before investing in any tree or shrub, ask some questions: how tall and wide will this grow? Many evergreens are slow growing, but eventually they can get quite large. Other trees may also grow larger than you expect. Look at the final dimensions of any tree or shrub before you dig the hole. Do you want a deciduous tree, one that gives cool shade in the summer months and then loses its leaves come fall? Make sure the tree or shrub you're planting is the right one for the spot you have in mind. A few things to consider:

- Does it have an invasive root structure? Then don't plant it too close to the house or driveway.
- How much water will it need?
- Will it give too much or too little shade for the location?
- Am I planting it too close to power lines? Look up before you plant.

Consider gentle fencing for garden definition

Surround your garden with a split rail or picket fence, not to keep out animals as we discussed before, but to define your space. If you use this garden plan, you would probably want to build a fence in a square along the edges of the property, or to separate the garden from the rest of your landscape. Bury chicken wire or hardware cloth at the base of fencing to keep unwanted animals at bay.

What kinds of fencing? Split rail, wattle fencing or stone walls harken back to rural spaces. White picket fences are pure cottage romance. Think of how many picket fences you've seen pinned on Pinterest.

Design inspiration

Pinterest is one of my favorite hobbies, an easy to way to keep track of garden and design ideas via virtual bulletin boards. I used it to find my vegetable garden's color palette. It influenced my choice of a red fountain as my kitchen garden's centerpiece. You'll see photos of my vegetable garden on pages 51 and 53.

In this chapter's garden design I've left room for a focal point at the center. You could place a birdbath (use a bubbler to really attract birds), fire pit, fountain, sundial, etc. You're only limited by your own imagination. Pinterest would be a good place to start discerning what you'd most enjoy. One more thing: Pinterest is a great tool, but it's another hobby that needs a timer set before you start. Otherwise, you may pin the day away. I wouldn't say that if I didn't have first-hand experience.

Sensual Flowers for Every Garden

Sweetly Scented

⇨ **ROSES:** especially heirloom varieties like 'Dame de Coeur,' 'Madame Isaac Pereire,' 'Zephirine Drouhin' and 'Duchesse de Brabant.' Old garden roses – also called antiques or heirlooms – grow in a more romantic growth habit. Before adding any rose to your garden, talk with local experts regarding which roses perform in your area. Note: 'Zephirine Drouhin' doesn't have prickles (thorns), so it's great around children.

⇨ **HELIOTROPE:** vanilla or cherry scented.

⇨ **EVENING-SCENTED STOCK:** one of my fave flowers to smell.

⇨ **PANSIES AND VIOLETS, A.K.A. VIOLAS:** cheerful faces, sweetly scented, with an iron constitution in chilly weather.

⇨ **FOUR O'CLOCKS:** can be grown from seed or tubers. The bright pink, heirloom variety is most fragrant in my garden. Their scent follows me throughout the garden in early evening.

⇨ **GARDEN PINKS:** 'Bath's Pink' is light purple and extremely fragrant with silver blue foliage.

⇨ **SWEET PEAS:** highly scented and easy to grow in cooler climates.

⇨ **SWEET WILLIAM:** biennial, so it's a great plant to start from seed for blooms the following year; or, if you're in a hurry, buy plants already growing.

⇨ **GARDEN PHLOX:** a very sweet scent, especially older forms.

⇨ **MIGNONETTE:** extremely fragrant.

⇨ **LILACS:** a spring scent all their own.

Blooms of Excitement

⇨ **SUNFLOWERS:** all sizes – giant ones like 'Mammoth' or dwarf, fuzzy ones like 'Honey Bear'.

⇨ **ZINNIAS:** from old-fashioned Zinnia elegans to the more diminutive Z. haageana; are among the hardest working, fastest growing flowers. I always find space for some in my vegetable garden and the ornamental garden, too. If you want butterflies, grow zinnias.

⇨ **HOLLYHOCKS:** so beautiful and old fashioned. Some can be sown and flower in the same year in a long season. Most are biennial. They grow in the first year and bloom the second. Worth the wait.

Color me blue

Blue is the least common color in the garden. Perhaps blue flowers don't want to compete with the sky. There are some wonderful blue flowers though, and these are easy to grow.

⇨ **CORNFLOWER OR BACHELOR'S BUTTON:** a cheerful annual of the most beautiful blue. You can direct sow outdoors in shades of light to dark blue. Watch out for seed mixes though, because they often have white and pink mixed in.

⇨ **MORNING GLORY:** 'Heavenly Blue' is the most perfect shade of sky. They have a tough seed coat so soak seeds in water or manure tea for 24 hours to make them sprout earlier and grow faster.

⇨ **BLUESTAR:** a group of perennials that bloom in soft shades of light blue in spring against light green foliage. This same foliage turns bright yellow in fall and is considered one of our best fall natives.

⇨ **SALVIA:** 'Victoria Blue' is often used in cottage garden settings, so it is at home in perennial beds and kitchen gardens. Although listed as an annual north of Zone 8, it usually overwinters in my Zone 7 garden.

⇨ **BORAGE:** an herb that is easy to grow from seed. Sow it directly into the garden and watch for fuzzy leaves to appear. While the leaves are quite coarse, the flowers emerge, nearly fairy-like, hanging downward to attract pollinators, especially fuzzy bumblebees. The flowers taste a bit like cucumbers and are great on salads. Pictured at right.

> **TIP:** Whatever you do, don't plant trumpet vine (Campsis radicans) or Japanese honeysuckle (Lonicera japonica) in your garden. While they may look sweet, they are actually beasties and will take over. Both are considered not only aggressive, but also invasive. Instead, plant native crossvine (Bignonia capreolata) or one of our native honeysuckles.

Adapting the design to your needs

Although this design does incorporate some herbs and vegetables, I've planted it primarily with simple enjoyment in mind. You may want to grow mostly vegetables here, instead. By now, you have a lot of experience thinking about and planning vegetable gardens. Where I've placed lamb's ear, for example, you could put another herb, like the creeping thyme in the other beds. Just keep size and shape in mind, whatever plants you choose. Another thought: you could plant more vegetables and herbs in the expansion parts of the garden, too. This would place vegetables on the outside, where they are more accessible – but you'll also want some type of fencing, because they won't be only accessible to you.

* * *

Way to go!

I hope that even if you still grow primarily a vegetable plot, you'll add flowers for your inner child. While vegetable flowers are beautiful in their own right, flowers, along with trees and shrubs, add a depth and dimension to a garden that annual plants just can't. In the next chapter, we'll explore this further and talk about how design elements can increase your enjoyment of your garden space. I'll show you how to choose and construct paths to last for years. We'll discuss fountains, garden art and where to find inspiration. You've probably realized that once you start gardening, the garden becomes more than somewhere you grow plants to eat. It becomes your haven, your barrier against the world's stresses and strife. It may even become your favorite destination, a vacation spot *not* away from home.

Chapter Eight

Pathways, Garden Art and Relaxation

Here's where we look at creative ways to enhance your garden so it becomes the place everyone wants to spend time in - starting with how to make garden paths and then we'll talk about having fun with garden art and other shiny things. And we mustn't forget about making places for just sitting and doing nothing at all.

IN YOUR FIRST YEAR OF DESIGNING A GARDEN FOR THE SENSES, you focused on creating a warm, family-friendly environment that captures the imagination. You included fruit trees, plants with foliage that sways in the breeze and plants with touchable leaves that are fascinating and safe for children. Your garden is well on its way to becoming a true delight for the senses, but now you need to make sure that visitors (and you!) are able to enjoy it. That's why in this chapter I included some additions to the garden to transform it into a destina-

tion. Some of these ideas are simple and some require a bit of work, but all will invite you and your family to set aside distractions and simply enjoy your garden.

Down the garden path

Never underestimate the value of a good garden path. It invites the visitor in and provides an avenue to wander while seeing everything the garden has to offer. It also allows easy access to your plant beds. Paths can be earthy and picturesque or purely functional. No matter what, they should be smooth and easy to stroll. That will go a long way toward making your garden into a destination.

No more Bermuda grass! My original kitchen garden, built over 20 years ago, had a diamond-shaped raised bed in the center surrounded by four triangular beds. The paths between the beds were grass, and in my state, that means Bermuda grass. This tough turf is popular in much of the South because it's hard to kill even when faced with heat and drought. Bermuda spreads by underground roots, making it very difficult to keep in confined areas of a garden. Here in Oklahoma, I've fought Bermuda until my hands were sore, and it still snaked its way beneath the wood planks of my raised beds. Frankly, it drove me nuts.

After a few years, I could stand it no more. Lucky for me, I stumbled across the perfect solution when Bill and our son, Brennan, helped with an Eagle Scout project at a school for handicapped children. In an effort to make the pathways at the school wheelchair-accessible, the Boy Scouts swapped out the existing pea gravel with rubber mulch. Now, I usually abhor rubber mulch, but it was necessary to make the school garden accessible and safe for students. It also left a large amount of unwanted pea gravel. It was slated for the landfill – so instead, like so many things around here, we repurposed it.

Bill surprised me and brought the gravel home in a dump truck. This in itself wasn't surprising – I'm used to my true blue, tree-loving, paving contractor husband borrowing equipment from work. But I was seriously excited about the pea gravel. Bill and I quickly devised a plan to get rid of that nasty Bermuda grass for good.

When our pea gravel project was finished, we had a pretty, usable and low-maintenance garden path that invited visitors to stroll through our garden. Would you like to start a similar project in your yard? It's pretty straight-forward.

Here's how Bill and I did it:

First, we lined the existing paths with heavy-duty landscape fabric and edged the outside of the garden with green metal edging. Our raised beds were already edged in wood for the interior paths. If you're starting this project from scratch, make sure you complete this step; it will prevent intrusion from unwanted plant forms. You will get some weeds from seeds on the wind, but these are minor intruders.

Then we filled the space with the gravel. That took two days of hard labor.

The weight of the gravel snuffed out most of the Bermuda grass, but there were stragglers. We didn't use weed killer because chemicals would have upset the garden's balance (I was already gardening organically at this point). Instead, I used a small blowtorch – I kid you not. So long as you're careful, this unlikely tool can work wonders.

Maintaining the path can take some attention, but it's still less work than Bermuda grass. *Note:* pea gravel is an excellent seed-starting medium; any seed within a hundred yards finds its way into my garden paths. Most are easy to pull. However, I still employ the blowtorch in the summer, along with Burnout II organic weed killer.

Other materials for your paths

Pea gravel isn't the only option for filling in garden paths, and it's not ideal for every environment. Although I like my pea gravel, my garden is on a hill, and the gravel slides downward whenever we get rain. This can be frustrating if you don't have the time or inclination to redistribute the gravel every few weeks. Decomposed granite, which is now more readily available, would have been a better choice, as it doesn't slide out of place as easily. But I wasn't going to replace my pea gravel anytime soon. We had paid for it with our sweat equity.

Before adding paving of any kind to your garden paths, consider your options. Smooth paths that are easy to walk on (brick, permeable pavers or decomposed granite) are great choices.

Of course, if you have a river rock windfall, go for it. Natural materials are a wonderful, green alternative to impermeable pavement like concrete. Some people use natural bark mulch in their paths, adding more each season to freshen them. Eventually, the bottom layers break down into compost, an added advantage. Or you could use straw or pine needles. I do like straw in the vegetable bed, so long as I can find it without seed heads. When I use straw with seed heads, I sometimes have more wheat growing in my garden than anything else.

You can also follow our example and use repurposed material for your pathways. Years later, when we expanded the garden by adding the potager, we repurposed concrete paving bricks for free. This, like using the pea gravel left over from the Eagle Scout project, saved a lot of material from the dump. We augmented the repurposed concrete paving bricks with several red brick walkways that played well with the overall design. I did this because the potager is more formal than my other vegetable garden, and the brick lent it an extra touch of style.

My best advice about designing garden paths is: don't be overwhelmed. My path projects took time and were done over a number of seasons. With each change, I learned more about the garden – and myself. And don't worry about this being the final decision for your garden paths. Your needs will change. Now, I'm thinking about ways to reduce my work because I do the maintenance solo.

No water feature? No pool? No problem.

Our property backs up to a large pond. Beautiful, right? Too bad I never see it. This much-sought-after water feature is way down the hill from the garden, so I hardly notice it unless a visitor points it out. This has been a struggle for me because I need water in the garden; I love the sound it makes and the insects and animals it brings. I'd love a pool, but those things can be pricey and not always environmentally feasible. Thankfully, Pinterest showed me the solution.

I've always loved shiny surfaces, like glass and antique flow blue china. On various boards, I had been pinning blue and white china, blown glass, glazed ceramic fountains and swimming pools. Rearranging my boards one day, I unintentionally lined these up next to each other, and I discovered the connection: all of these items shone and shimmered like sunlight on still water. In a climate where rain often doesn't come for months on end, I need crystalline surfaces, because they emulate this play of light on water. Getting a pool isn't necessary – thank goodness – but having glass garden art is.

Shimmer and shine. I adopted this new idea with zeal. My garden is now decorated with beautiful pieces of glass art, my touchstone being blown glass in natural shapes of leaves and flowers. Your favorite style will probably be different, but regardless, incorporating glass into your garden will give it the lovely shimmer of water at rest.

Art in the Garden

This brings me to art. Art is in the eye of the beholder, and what you love may not be another's fashion. But who cares? It's your garden! The British landscape designer and photographer Fiona Heron sums it up for gardeners everywhere: "Trust your soul – ignore fashion."

If you get a chance to travel, visit arboretums and botanic gardens. Because they have the budgets to accommodate art and large-scale plantings, you may find art you fall for. If something seems beyond your pocketbook, ask for the name of the artist; they often do smaller works that are more affordable. Or, choose something similar that makes you smile. While you're there, you can also take photos of landscaping ideas you'd love to try in your own garden. Upload photos directly to Google for an image search of similar things. If you find something you like, you're in business.

Whenever I travel, I keep an eye out for interesting art pieces or inspiration for my garden back home. Through work, I am fortunate to travel to Seattle at least once a year. There is where I fell in love with blown glass, an art form that the city is known for. I always look up gardens and nurseries before I travel, too; using your network of gardening friends will help you discover unique and interesting places in every area of the country. Garden forums, blogs and Facebook pages devoted to a particular interest – like urban farming – are great ways to discover what you love. Google Groups and Hangouts, Pinterest and Twitter are also valuable resources. Take advantage of them before your next vacation. You never know what treasure you'll stumble upon that will be perfect in your garden.

Other art pieces, such as wind chimes, wind-motion art, glass surfaces and tumbling water, add elements of sensory pleasure to a garden. My sister loves wind chimes and has several on her porch where she has coffee each morning. They're part of her life every day. We should incorporate the things we love into the spaces where we live; they transform a house into a home, and a garden into a destination.

Stop and smell the roses...really

We should also give ourselves places to sit and rest. One of the great disadvantages to being a gardener is perfectionism. I must work on my compulsion to perfect the garden every time I go out there. I tell myself I'm just

going to have a cup of tea outside on the deck, and before long, I'm knee-deep in dirt. (I know, I know – I preach that we shouldn't aim for perfection. I'm working on it!) One way I combat this thinking is to give myself permission to sit and simply enjoy the garden.

I've placed fun seating that I love throughout the garden, and most of it is also meaningful. Near the potager sit two red, 1940s metal tubing chairs. They remind me of my grandparents and long summer nights when we children chased fireflies as the grownups talked. I found the eclectic set at at this wonderful and quirky vintage show called The Junk Hippy Roadshow. With a name like that, I knew it was going to be good. Don't worry, though, if similar shows don't stop in your town. You can also find chairs like these at antique stores or reproductions through Amazon.

In the lower garden, I have my mother's chairs. She gave them to me many years ago. Right now they're purple, but I've painted them nearly every color imaginable in the years they've lived here. I am a virtuoso with spray paint. No matter what color they are, these chairs are special to me because of our shared history. My mom really enjoys seeing what color I'll paint them next.

So, plan for seating and then take a seat. It's part of that whole "being in the moment" thing that we know is good for us but keep failing to live by. You try, and I'll try. We'll keep each other honest. Resting should be part of gardening, too.

* * *

Way to go!

While the paths in life and gardening are never straight and completely weed free, you and I have come a long way in this book, from containers on a balcony to this beautiful and peaceful refuge, your third garden. We've seen this garden through two years, and there's a third year ahead. More to think about and do...and find contentment in.

Chapter Nine

Caring for the Soil...and Yourself

Going into our third year, I want to help you think more about gardening as a process and not a series of to-do lists. Let's turn the idea of "chores" (even weeding) into a meditation that benefits your entire life and your garden's. I'll be offering further thoughts on gardening organically, caring for your soil, attracting pollinators and getting comfortable with the "good bugs" in your garden.

OUR LIVES SHOULD EBB AND FLOW WITH PHYSICAL WORK AND REST. Gardening, while fun, involves physical work. Still, it's a blessed sort of work. Garden chores aren't like household ones. Why do you think so many cleaning products have scents to remind you of the outdoors? On a perfect spring or fall day, isn't that where we all want to be? No one I know actually loves doing the laundry or paying bills (although we like the results).

Weeding, on the other hand, restores both you and your garden, especially once you work with improved soil that is easy to dig. Garden chores have a rhythm all their own. While they can be repetitive, they also free your mind from the daily grind. Every day in the garden is different from the one before. You see different creatures…the plants grow and change. Garden tasks of raking, weeding, digging, planting and sowing tie us to our earliest human roots and create a sense of relaxation.

Weeding as meditation

A very wise woman once told me that I lived too much in my head. She said I let ideas swirl about, tumbling and turning, causing me extra stress. Her advice? I needed to get outside and move my body so my mind could have a rest.

When I am stuck on a writing project – yes, writers are often stuck – I do one of two things. If I don't have much time, I grab a broom and sweep the kitchen floor. My desk is in the kitchen, so the broom is always handy. Repetitive movement of the body is great rest for your aching mind. If I have more time, I head outside and weed a small section of the garden. Weeding is a great and gentle form of exercise and meditation. I set a timer so I won't stay out there all day if I'm working on deadline. Since I garden mostly in raised beds, I'm able to work on a bed or two at a time.

Thinking in "zones". I see my entire garden as separate zones. The back garden was once my kitchen garden, but it is now a mixed perennial border. It has four long beds: two diamond-shaped beds with eight smaller triangles. I know it sounds large, but it's manageable because I break it into four zones. I work in zone 1 first and then move on to zone 2 and so on. Since I mulch all of my beds two times a year, I actually don't have to work very hard. The soil is soft and nice to work with. In the spring, I use shredded leaves and compost for mulch. These break down quickly because of summer heat and earthworms in action. In the fall, I mulch the garden with shredded pine bark to overwinter. In the vegetable gardens, I mulch with straw most years. I let this break down, turning it over come spring. Earthworms do much of the work for me, making the soil soft, friable and easy to dig and weed.

Compost, Compost, Compost

Gardeners who grow organically know that healthy soil means you have less disease in the garden, stronger plants and less insect damage. Compost is key. It's like lubricant in a car engine; it keeps everything running smoothly.

Improve your soil, improve your life

Why compost? Adding compost and other natural matter improves soil composition, moisture retention and fertility. It makes the soil richer and looser. Plant roots don't struggle going into the ground, and they take up soil nutrients better. Also, you don't have to work as hard to dig and weed. Everybody is happy.

There are as many ways to compost as there are gardeners. Every gardener has his or her own special recipe. I take the laissez-faire approach first championed by Cassandra Danz, a.k.a. Mrs. Greenthumbs, a great gardener and comedian, who taught me a lot about letting go. This is about the simplest composting recipe you can find.

Two kinds of things go into a compost pile:

⇨ **GREEN MATTER:** untreated grass and plant clippings, small weeds without seeds and leftover plant material from your kitchen. Don't put meat or dairy in your pile because animals may be attracted to it, and it smells bad as it decays.

⇨ **BROWN MATTER:** leaves, coffee grounds, tea leaves, eggshells, small twigs, dried weeds and other garden refuse.

The smaller the pieces you place in the pile, the faster it all breaks down. Don't put any diseased plants in your compost pile because that will spread disease around your garden.

Mrs. Greenthumbs' Compost Recipe

Step 1: In a corner of the garden, start your pile by alternating layers of brown matter and green matter.

Step 2: Top off the pile with brown matter and a bit of soil (the soil is to avoid a smelly pile).

Step 3: Water the pile until it is saturated top to bottom. This may take some time because piles compress as they grow larger, and water may run off the sides.

Step 4: Leave it to rot. I said it was simple!

This is not what's called hot composting. It is not fast, and it won't break down weed seeds. It is, however, the way Mother Nature makes compost, and her way is good enough for me. Think of forests: leaves fall from the trees; plants die at the beginning of winter and crumple. Over time, everything rots and turns into wonderful compost.

You may have heard about the need to turn a compost pile frequently, to let in air and keep the temperature even. That's fine if you want to speed up the process. I rarely turn my compost pile, but I do water it once a week in summer since my area mostly sees rain only in spring and fall. If your pile is too dry, the microbes can't do their work, and they are primarily the ones who break down your pile into black gold. For those of you in rainy climates, your experience may differ. A pile that is too wet or has too much green matter is out of balance and will smell "off."

I also have a sturdy mesh compost bin that sits on one side of the garden for easy access. Nobody wants to cart garden refuse very far to dump it. I've found that if I want to keep making compost, I need the process to be easy for me. This bin's dark color absorbs heat from the sun, and the mesh allows good air circulation.

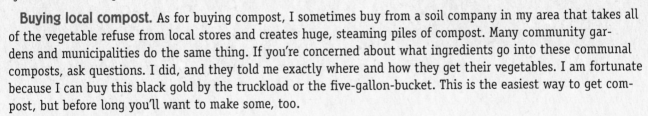

If you want to take the hot approach, there is plenty of great information online. And you can find a large array of composting systems – like compost tumblers, which are pricey, but great tools if you use them.

Buying local compost. As for buying compost, I sometimes buy from a soil company in my area that takes all of the vegetable refuse from local stores and creates huge, steaming piles of compost. Many community gardens and municipalities do the same thing. If you're concerned about what ingredients go into these communal composts, ask questions. I did, and they told me exactly where and how they get their vegetables. I am fortunate because I can buy this black gold by the truckload or the five-gallon-bucket. This is the easiest way to get compost, but before long you'll want to make some, too.

The matter of manure

It's hard to believe, but animal manure has become controversial recently. There are three reasons why:

○ *Overuse of antibiotics and other medications in animals (along with the factory farm method).*
○ *Salmonella scares from tainted food bought at grocery stores.*
○ *Persistent herbicides that remain in an animal's gut even after digestion.*

No wonder people are concerned about using manure on their gardens.

Chicken manure. I do use manure on my garden, but it is all locally sourced from my very own chickens that aren't vaccinated or given antibiotics. Chicken manure contains more nitrogen than other manures, so it must be set aside for about six months before being placed on the garden. I pile mine near the barn, away from the house. If you're concerned about using manure from vaccinated animals or those that forage on sprayed fields, find a local source for manure that you trust. You can also fertilize your garden by other methods.

To learn more about using manure safely, see the Resources page.

Saving pollinators and other creatures

Part of keeping the garden healthy is also taking care of the creatures that live, procreate and die there. This may surprise you, but I was once terrified of bugs and insects, especially flying ones. I hated when moths and brown beetles would fling themselves at my porch light on summer nights. Invariably, I would go outside and one of them would accidentally fling itself on *me*.

It may sound naïve, but I didn't realize bugs were part of the bargain when I began gardening. I just wanted vegetables, roses and other flowers. I saw insects as adversaries and nothing more – showing just how influenced I once was by advertising. Thank goodness I educated myself and don't think that way anymore.

A garden without insects, lizards, toads and other creatures is a chemically-sprayed garden. It is as unnatural as a day without birdsong. I now find the creatures living in my garden as interesting as the plants I grow. They bring so much life to the garden, I find myself planting things specifically for them to munch on.

If you plant it, they will come

Although I had gardened organically for years, I made things formal in 2009 when I applied to the National Wildlife Federation for my garden to become a Certified Wildlife Habitat. After looking at their requirements, I added several creature amenities to make my landscape more inviting to insects and animals. This year, I upgraded my habitat to a bird-friendly one by adding plants specifically beloved by birds for food and shelter. Also, after reading about the seriously declining number of bumblebees, I became a member of the Xerces Society for Invertebrate Conservation. My garden is now registered as a pollinator habitat with the Xerces Society too.

A Garden for Butterflies

If you're scared of insects (like I was), start with butterflies. Most of us like butterflies. If you want them to visit, you need to grow nectar plants for the adults and host plants for their caterpillars in or near your vegetable garden. Even the Smithsonian has a butterfly habitat garden in the center of Washington, D.C.

To get you started, here are three types of butterflies commonly found across North America:

⇨ **SWALLOWTAILS:** Among the largest of butterflies, Swallowtails capture our imagination with their winged flight and beautiful coloration. They are very easy to attract to your yard. Adults love perennial garden phlox. Caterpillars like to eat dill, parsley and fennel. They are voracious around dill, so plant several groupings to keep them (and yourself) satisfied.

⇨ **MONARCHS:** Once common, this species is now in trouble due to loss of habitat and cold weather in Mexico, where they overwinter. Planting milkweed in your garden can help save the Monarchs. Since awareness has spread, you can now easily find many types of milkweed. Choose one native to your area, if possible, and contact your local native plant society or butterfly enthusiasts for places to buy it.

⇨ **GULF FRITILLARIES:** Adults are pretty easy to please. They, like all butterflies, enjoy flowers with simple structures, such as zinnias, pentas, purple coneflowers, etc. These caterpillars eat passionflower vine with what can only be described as passion. I grow two hardy passionflower vines up one side of my deck just for these butterflies.

Chrysalis alert

In fall, watch out for butterfly chrysalises, a.k.a. "chrysalides". Although we tend to be familiar with the Monarch's showy green and gold chrysalis, other butterflies have a chrysalis that can resemble dead leaves. Always be careful in the garden, because many other insects have laid their eggs, too. Every action in the garden, no matter how small, affects it in some way, sometimes for good and other times not so good.

The best thing about growing a garden where butterflies are welcome is the balance it creates. If you let one creature in, other good things follow. It's a little like opening your heart to good things in the world.

Pollinator appreciation

Pollinators are just one of the many good things. They make it possible for you to grow squash, pumpkins and loads of other great vegetables. And the flowers! That's one happy bee about to land on the coneflower in the photo.

Without pollinators, the garden is a boring place. What would we do without fat bumblebees, soaring butterflies and flower flies? Yes, there are such things as flower flies, a.k.a. hover flies In fact, much of the world's plants are pollinated by these creatures that are often mistaken for wasps or bees! When you see a creature sipping nectar from a blossom, don't grab a can of Raid. Instead, sit on the ground and enjoy the show. If you plant flowers with simple structures, you'll discover just how many different flying creatures pollinate your garden.

Did you know insects won't bother you when they are feeding? Whether they are wasps, bees or other pollinators, they are far too busy eating and pollinating to sting – unless, of course, you grab them with your hand. You can work in the garden quite peacefully with most creatures even the stinging ones.

A plea for spiders

Did you read *Charlotte's Web* in school? Did you know that the author, E.B. White, was married to an avid gardener, Katharine White? When Charlotte tells us her full name is Charlotte A. Cavatica, she is letting us know she's a barn spider *(Araneus cavaticus)*. While I love all of my pollinators, garden spiders (including barn spiders like Charlotte) are special favorites. Not only are they fascinating and mostly harmless to humans, but they also reduce the population of chomping insects in the garden.

A friend visited recently and asked me why there were so many spiders in my garden. I told her that it was spider season. Common garden spiders have their own seasons, just like flowers and other plants. The spiders called *Argiope aurantia,* in the photos at right, are more visible in my garden in late summer and early fall, with their large yellow and black bodies and expansive webs. I know it's not pleasant to walk into one of their webs, but next time, think how hard they work in the garden and watch out for them.

For information on other pollinators, please visit the websites listed on the Resources page. The more you learn about the ways that nature works in harmony, the more you'll want to protect it. How do I know?

It's what happened to me.

Way to go!

I hope that no matter what type of garden you plant and grow, you take a little something from each of the gardens and chapters we've spent time with in this book. Think of those things you love most about the places you've visited and lived. Make a mosaic of memory, either online or in a journal. When you're

incorporating a new bed or something artful in your backyard, don't neglect your five senses. We don't just see the garden; we touch, smell and hear it too. Whatever says home to you and makes you feel whole at the end of the day is what you should have in your sanctuary, your home and garden.

Next, we're going to visit with other gardeners who work in concert to create a symphony of community garden goodness. Although you may be satisfied working in your garden alone, you may find that certain obstacles keep you from

growing all you want or need. Or, perhaps, you want to share your bounty and work alongside others. If so, the next chapter is the one for you. Even if you never garden in community, I think you'll find these gardeners are inspiring.

Chapter Ten

Gardening in Community

A look at three kinds of community gardens and how they are changing urban and suburban life for the better.

WHY WOULD YOU WANT TO GROW PLANTS WITH A GROUP OF PEOPLE YOU HARDLY KNOW, in someplace other than your own home? I can think of at least five reasons:

1. Perhaps, to make friends or gain knowledge.

2. You want to grow more than you can on your balcony and patio.

3. Your neighborhood association covenants or municipal ordinances don't allow for front yard garden expression.

4. Your yard is too shady for vegetable production.

5. You're an extrovert.

Lucky for you, in nearly every city, town and village across the country, community gardens bloom with vibrant good health. Not only can you socialize as you grow, you also benefit by learning about your climate and growing conditions from gardeners nearby who care.

Become neighbors again

Community gardens sport names like Sunfield, Sunshine and Commonwealth. They are a heritage from long-ago years when we gardened together in our neighborhoods. Community gardens are a way to recreate that neighborly life – a way to bring back the meaning of "neighbor": the one who chats with you over the fence, the one who sweats with you as you sow more seeds.

These gardens are a wealth of information and fun. Most garden organizers see part of their role as catalysts to make the world a better place through education and great food. Gardeners in cities are leading the way by rehabbing vacant lots and remediating urban soils from chemical toxins. They also gather leftover vegetables from local stores and restaurants and make compost. It's one more way to keep refuse out of our overburdened garbage system and return it to the soil. You can't help but be inspired. This is community giving, and growing, at its best and most basic.

Learn from experts

To get a sense of how gardening in community can differ from place to place, I spoke with three gardeners who grow in three different garden movements. One is a neighborhood development that includes a garden at its center for homeowners. The second is a city-wide garden transformation, and the third is a traditional community garden that morphed into an urban park on donated land. Two are in Texas, one is in Chicago.

A neighborhood garden in a planned community

After a stint in AmeriCorps, 34-year-old Colleen Dieter started her own landscape business. Her work focuses on customers who have complicated landscapes and who need knowledgeable care for Texas' harsh climate. In 2011, the developers of Sunfield, a master planned community in Buda, Texas hired Colleen. Sunfield is a neighborhood with something different, as they describe it, and her expertise fit well with their vision. Sunfield's design incorporated a small orchard of fig and pear trees, along with vegetable plots for any resident who wanted to "adopt" one. Sunfield also grows demonstration plots where gardeners experiment with techniques and different types of seeds. Any extra food the residents grow in the demonstration and adopted plots is donated to local food pantries.

Colleen manages the demonstration gardens, teaches vegetable gardening classes and is a resource for the gardeners, along with the garden, making sure everything runs smoothly. She also maintains Sunfield's blog, a great way for the gardening neighbors to exchange tips and support each other's work. Many community gardens have websites; you can get a feel for a particular garden from their online presence.

Colleen's Tips

○ **Have enough time to donate to your plot and the garden. It's not like going out your back door in your PJs to water. Most community gardens require some volunteer hours too. These are a great way to get to know your neighbors and other members of the community.**

○ **Factor driving into your plans. You will probably need to drive to most community gardens.**

While community gardeners are excellent resources of inspiration and gardening know-how, members also depend upon you to uphold your end of the garden and be responsible for your plot.

Before you join, ask if the garden has a tool library and know when it's open. Carting tools back and forth in your car gets old fast.

Citywide urban gardening and the new Victory Gardens

LaManda Joy started the Peterson Garden Project in 2010 after seeing a black and white photograph of a WWII garden on Peterson Avenue in Chicago. LaManda later discovered that the land from the photograph, located at Peterson and Campbell, was up for sale. Through her alderman, she contacted the owner, who agreed to a garden on the vacant property. Thus, the Peterson Garden was born, which now has 212 raised bed vegetable plots, filled with compost and tended by the many gardeners who have adopted them. This garden led to the "Project," where gardeners attempted to create gardens throughout the city based upon methods used in WWII Victory Gardens. Soon, LaManda had gardens popping up all over the Chicago area, especially apropos for a city incorporated under the Latin phrase, *Urbs in Horto,* meaning "city in a garden."

To carry her message more widely, LaManda dresses as Rosie the Riveter and speaks to communities across the country about Victory Gardens. Her book, *Start a Community Food Garden: the Essential Handbook,* is designed for those desiring the know-how to organize their own community gardens, and to give information about growing in existing gardens.

LaManda's Tips

○ Find an existing garden and grow there for a season before attempting to build another. Gardeners may find the garden where they're growing can best benefit from their enthusiasm.

○ If a group of community gardeners is determined to do their own thing, she suggests they find a local organization responsible for community gardens. It might be a not-for-profit, municipal group (like a city parks district or other entity) or a government agency. Every place is different, but do some research and find out what resources are available before you dig.

○ Be open to new experiences. The community is sometimes better than the gardening itself. There are ideas and experts galore, and you can meet people who become lifelong friends. Community gardens are the great common denominator – the sun shines on everyone, rain falls on everyone . . . it's a great way to feel connected to nature and your small patch of Earth.

"Gardeners, scholars say, are the first sign of commitment to a community."

– Anne Raver

An urban oasis

Randy Thompson and Janet Adams are longtime volunteers at Sunshine Community Gardens, an urban oasis in the center of Austin, Texas, on land owned by the Texas School for the Blind and Visually Impaired. It has 150 plots on 4 acres of land. Sunshine Community Gardens is green space in the center of city life. People from neighboring offices eat lunch in the gardens and treat them like a city park.

Randy and Janet's Tips

○ **Get on a waiting list at the end of the growing season. Sunshine usually has a waiting list of a year to get a single plot.**

○ **Think of what you want to grow in terms of what you eat at home. You won't keep up with your garden if you don't like to eat the produce.**

○ **You don't have the power to change the world. You do have the power to change your actions to effect change on an individual level. Joining a community garden can do just that.**

Community gardens like Sunshine are places of innovation. They try new ideas and solutions. They are usually game for experimenting with new types of planting styles, too. Randy is in charge of seed ordering for the garden. He's discovered through trial and error that birds and other urban wildlife are most attracted to red tomatoes so he orders seed for drought tolerant varieties in colors usually other than red. Randy also came up with an ingenious way to water tomatoes and other thirsty vegetables. He buries soaker hoses in the ground and places tomato roots near the leaky hose. Water goes directly to the plant's roots without waste.

Janet has been president of the garden and now serves as vice president. Here's what she tells prospective gardeners: You aren't renting a plot, you are joining a community.

That sense of community is at the heart of gardening together. When you decide to join a group of gardeners – or one or two groups – you get so much more than zucchini and tomatoes. You become part of a family of volunteers who want to make the world a better place.

Seven Habits of Gardeners Who Care

Are you worried about the climate and Mother Earth? Do you want to help the planet? While we can't do everything, we can always do something. Here are seven simple garden practices to improve our planet's complexion, one garden at a time.

1. **Say no to chemical pesticides.** If you have a bug problem, your garden isn't balanced. If you spray pesticides, even natural ones, you're upsetting the delicate ecosystem even further. Look to my suggestions on dealing with common insects. Although I do use natural pesticides, it's rare. It took more than a season or two, but my vegetable garden is now mostly in balance, and good bugs take care of bad ones.

2. **Say no to chemical herbicides.** Weeds are going to pop up. After all, you're making such a nice home for them to blow into, and weeds are just plants. As with bugs, we don't want in our gardens, start with the easiest and least harmful action first. Pull weeds at their smallest. Reach down close to the soil at the base of the weed and give a tug. Some weeds come up easily. Others are more difficult because they have spreading roots or tap roots. Boiling water works on many weeds. If you must use an herbicide, try one of the natural ones in the sources list or make your own. Look for those that are OMRI listed (the Organic Materials Review Institute). Note, though, that natural herbicides tend to kill everything in their path. They don't know the difference between bindweed and a morning glory like 'Heavenly Blue.'

3. **Learn how to compost, or buy some that's organic.** Compost is food for the soil. Although I compost, I can never make enough for my garden, so I also buy some every year. I also use leaves as mulch for the garden, letting them decay over winter.

4. Keep it clean. This may sound crazy when you're up to your ears in dirt, but keep the ground beneath your plants clean of dropped vegetables, diseased leaves or fruit. Throw the veggies and fruit into your compost pile, but anything with disease needs to leave the premises. At the end of the season, also clean up any leftover refuse so pathogens don't have time to spread. And pull any weeds before they spread seeds over winter. A clean garden is a happy one.

5. Mulch. Mulch is a blanket for plants. In the winter, it keeps soil toasty warm around their roots. In the summer, it keeps roots cool. Only use natural mulches and say no to rubber mulch. It won't break down and make the ground more fertile. Natural wood mulches and other things like pecan hulls, shredded leaves, grass clippings and straw all make good mulch. I live in a wooded area, and I prize my shredded leaf piles as the best mulch I can't buy. You don't even need to shred the leaves of some trees because they will decay in place, though oak leaves are made of tougher stuff and need shredding.

6. Grow native plants for your area. Natives are important. They often have simple flowers that pollinators can't resist. So, next to that tomato, grow something blooming that's native, too. Talk to local experts and plant native flowers that do well in your county. What's native in one area isn't always native in another.

7. Conserve water. Water is our most valuable resource. Treat it as such. We've all seen sprinkler systems watering during a rainstorm, and that's a waste. Water in the morning and use drip irrigation in drier regions of the country. Perhaps, get a rain barrel or two. It's the little things that make a garden grow.

One last thing . . .

While no book of this size can cover everything about gardening, I hope you now feel you can grow whatever you want, from great food to beautiful, pollinator-friendly flowers and savory herbs. Gardening is mysterious because we're dealing with eternal Earthly truths. That is part of its allure, and why I'm still amazed by what unfurls from a single seed.

Gardening is also craft – homemaking in its truest sense. To grow something and eat it is a fundamental pleasure and skill so many of us are missing. But it's like riding a bike: once you know how, you simply know, and no one can ever take that away from you. My dad always said education was the key to the good life. Now I know how right he was.

We began where all good things start, at the beginning. We learned to start small. We filled the best containers for our climate with potting soil and grew some beautiful and tasty veggies. We learned about crop rotation and how to wisely water with drip irrigation. We built upon our successes and gained knowledge from any crop failures or planting mistakes. Process over perfection became our watchword, and we became more confident each year.

Here's the truth. There is no need for fancy contraptions or acres of space. No matter where you call home, you can garden. Whether it's in your front or backyard or even within a community setting, your patch of Earth is yours for the sowing. You now have a blueprint to make raised beds if you want and garden plans for each type of garden I've discussed.

I'd love to hear from you. Tell me how you've implement these ideas and made them your own. Feel free to share your experiences and questions on my Facebook page or the 20-30 Something Garden Guide blog.

Don't forget to plant what you love to eat and what pollinators love to sip from, too. Try new varieties; try heirlooms. Make every season count – and no matter what happens, enjoy each day. You're in the garden after all. You're home.

Dee

"Everything that slows us down and forces patience, everything that sets us back into the slow circles of nature, is a help. Gardening is an instrument of grace."

– May Sarton

RESOURCES

Garden diary supplies
- **Rite in the Rain notebooks and all weather pens:** http://www.riteintherain.com/

Community Gardens mentioned in the book
- **Sunfield,** http://www.sunfieldtx.com
- **Commonwealth Urban Farms of OKC,** http://commonwealthurbanfarms.com/
- **Sunshine Community Garden,** http://www.sunshinecommunitygarden.org/

The Matter of Manure
- **Factory Farm Map:** http://www.factoryfarmmap.org/problems/
- **"Using Manure Safely in Gardens,"** University of Maine Extension Publications, http://umaine.edu/publications/2510e/
- **"Using Animal Manure as Fertilizer,"** University of Florida IFAS Extension, http://gardeningsolutions.ifas.ufl.edu/giam/maintenance_and_care/soil_fertilizer_and_nutrients/manure.html
- **Authentic Haven Brand Manure Tea,** http://www.manuretea.com/

Saving pollinators and other creatures
- **Xerces Society for Invertebrate Conservation,** http://www.xerces.org/
- **National Wildlife Federation,** http://www.nwf.org/
- **"Butterfly Gardening,"** Missouri Botanical Garden, http://www.missouribotanicalgarden.org/visit/family-of-attractions/butterfly-house/butterflies-and-plants/butterfly-gardening.aspx
- **Smithsonian Butterfly Habitat Garden,** http://www.gardens.si.edu/our-gardens/butterfly-habitat-garden.html
- **Butterflies of the World Foundation,** http://www.botwf.org/index.html

INDEX

INDEX

ACKNOWLEDGMENTS

"Friends... they cherish one another's hopes. They are kind to one another's dreams."

– Henry David Thoreau

Writing is a solitary job in many ways, but we need the help of our friends and family, who nourish us and take up the slack, when our brains are mush, and our fingers cramp.

I want to first thank the love of my life, my husband, Bill, who helps me build all of my crazy garden projects and who indulges my every garden whim, whether it's making another garden plot, raising a flock of chickens, constructing a greenhouse and maybe, next year, even getting honeybees.

Thank you to my children, Ashley, Megan, Brennan and Claire, for letting me have the time and peace of mind to write down what's in my heart. This book contains so much of your spirits because I thought of each of you as I wrote it. These are the lessons we both learned as you toddled through the garden soil after me.

To Aimee Ryan, who helped guide my children and who is the best friend a girl could ever have. I don't know what I would do without your can-do spirit. I tip my teacup to you.

To my mother, Rose, who taught me anything worth doing was worth doing right and who is my biggest fan. In my eyes, you're like your namesake, crimson haired and fair as the morning dawn.

To Debra Prinzing, for always lending a listening ear and a guiding voice as we travel along life's garden path. Thank you especially for encouraging me to blog and find my voice. Whenever I think of the Bloedel Reserve and walking in the rain, I think of you.

To Sharon Lovejoy, who mentored me from afar when I was a young mother. Your books on gardening with children became our travel guides as we raised sunflower houses and planted hollyhocks for dolls' dresses. Through our blogs, we've become dear friends. I appreciate your guidance and wisdom in the writing process.

To my writing and gardening group, the Plurkettes, for their sage advice on all matters garden and life related. Thank you for ideas, photos, and for being there every single day when I switch on the computer.

To all of my other friends, online and off, who helped me write these growing lessons, who searched for photographs when I needed them, who reached across the miles and held my hand – I can't tell you how much you mean to me. I especially want to thank Annie Haven, Helen Weis, Shawna Coronado, Linda Lehmusvirta, Riz Reyes, Leslie Bennett, Stefani Bittner, Colleen Dieter, Lynn Felici-Gallant, LaManda Joy, Marie Wreath, Barbara Van Gorder and Randy Thompson. If I forgot anyone, please forgive me.

To everyone at St. Lynn's Press – Paul, Cathy, Holly, Allison and Claire – thank you for helping me bring this book to fruition. I'm grateful for your support and kindness. Thank you for listening to my ideas and then making them better.

Finally, I want to thank my Grandma Nita, who taught me how to love the dirt, flowers, and even bugs. I still miss you, but I'll meet you in the eternal garden one day.

ABOUT THE AUTHOR

DEE NASH IS A PROFESSIONAL WRITER, SPEAKER AND GARDENER, born and raised in Oklahoma. She lives with her husband and children on 7.5 acres between the Great American Prairie and the beginnings of the deciduous forest – along with animals Maddie the Wonder Dog, Tap, her chocolate Labrador, two rescue cats, Sophie and Tricksy, and twenty chickens, mostly unnamed. Dee gardens on an acre or so and grows everything she can, including vegetables, roses, daylilies, native plants and other favorite perennials, trees and shrubs.

A frequent contributor of writing and photography to *Oklahoma Gardener* magazine, her writing has appeared in *Organic Gardening, Fine Gardening, flower* magazine, The Oklahoman, the Oklahoma Horticultural Society's *Horticulture Horizons,* and *The Daylily Journal.* She also writes for Fiskars Corporation. Dee is a member of the Garden Writers Association, the Oklahoma Horticultural Society and Great Garden Speakers.

Follow Dee online at:

Website/Blog: http://reddirtramblings.com, http://20-30somethinggardenguide.com/ and http://deenash.com

Facebook: https://www.facebook.com/DeeANash

Twitter: https://twitter.com/#!/reddirtramblin

Pinterest: http://pinterest.com/deeanash/

YouTube: Nash Garden